Displaying
Your Findings

Displaying Your Findings

A Practical Guide for Creating Figures, Posters, and Presentations

Adelheid A. M. Nicol and Penny M. Pexman

American Psychological Association • *Washington, DC*

Printed in the United States of America
First Printing January 2003
Second Printing August 2003
Third Printing January 2005

Published by
American Psychological Association
750 First Street, NE
Washington, DC 20002
www.apa.org

To order
APA Order Department
P.O. Box 92984
Washington, DC 20090-2984
Tel: (800) 374-2721; Direct: (202) 336-5510
Fax: (202) 336-5502; TDD/TTY: (202) 336-6123
Online: www.apa.org/books/
Email: order@apa.org

In the U.K., Europe, Africa, and the Middle East, copies may be ordered from
American Psychological Association
3 Henrietta Street
Covent Garden, London
WC2E 8LU England

Typeset in Adobe Minion and Helvetica by Kachergis Book Design, Pittsboro, NC

Printer: Automated Graphic Systems, White Plains, MD
Cover Designer: Naylor Design, Washington, DC
Technical/Production Editor: Jennifer L. Zale

The opinions and statements published are the responsibility of the authors, and such opinions and statements do not necessarily represent the policies of the American Psychological Association.

LIBRARY OF CONGRESS CATALOGING-IN-PUBLICATION DATA

Nicol, Adelheid A. M.
  Displaying your findings : a practical guide for creating figures, posters, and presentations / Adelheid A.M. Nicol & Penny M. Pexman.
     p. cm.
Includes index.
  ISBN 1-55798-978-8 (alk. paper)
  1. Psychological literature. 2. Psychology—Graphic methods. 3. Psychology—Posters. 4. Poster presentations I. Pexman, Penny M. II. Title.

BF76.8 .N53 2003
150'.7'28—dc21

2002011969

British Library Cataloguing-in-Publication Data
A CIP record is available from the British Library.

Contents

Acknowledgments

In writing this book, we received assistance from many people. We extend special thanks to Yves Mayrand and Dave Pexman for their support; Ariane Mayrand Nicol, whose impending birth helped Adelheid keep on track and finish the book in a timely fashion; Michael Goodchild for advice about chapter 10; and John and Kate Pexman for providing drawings of scary monsters for chapter 5.

Displaying
Your Findings

CHAPTER 1

Introduction

Our first book, *Presenting Your Findings: A Practical Guide for Creating Tables,*[1] provided examples and specified important elements of effective tables. We wrote the book because, as graduate students and then as new faculty members, we had often struggled to figure out the best way to present our findings in tables. Since that book was published in 1999, several individuals have contacted us, wondering whether the same type of book existed for figures. In response, we have written the present book, hoping once again to facilitate the process of presenting research findings.

This book guides readers in designing figures following the guidelines of the fifth edition of the *Publication Manual of the American Psychological Association* (APA).[2] It does so by providing numerous examples of figures constructed to accompany fictional studies. We describe the studies in sufficient detail to illustrate how the figures were created. In the same manner, we also illustrate the preparation of effective posters and visual aids for conference presentations. We

1. Nicol, A. A. M., & Pexman, P. M. (1999). *Presenting your findings: A practical guide for creating tables.* Washington, DC: American Psychological Association.

2. American Psychological Association. (2001). *Publication manual of the American Psychological Association* (5th ed.). Washington, DC: Author.

hope that this method of describing the development of figures and conference materials will inspire researchers to be creative in producing clear, rich, and concise presentations of their results.

When to Use a Figure

Figures can be extremely helpful to a reader. They can be used to simplify complex information that would be difficult or lengthy to express in words, such as structural equation models, apparatus, or results. Figures can summarize or emphasize certain findings, illustrate complicated results such as interaction effects, and show patterns of data. They may also be used to demonstrate a progression of results such as trends or to accentuate a crucial point or change in the results. The goal of using figures is to help the reader better understand the material and grasp its essential aspects.

Authors should not use any figure that does not contribute to the reader's understanding of the information or that is redundant with the text. Figures that are too complicated and would require a lot of explanation should not be used. Furthermore, if a figure does not appear professional (either hand drawn by a professional or created with the use of a software program), then it is best not to include it.

Anatomy of a Figure

All figures consist of both the visual image to be presented (i.e., graph, plot, drawing, chart, or photograph) and the caption. In addition, sometimes a legend is included to help the reader interpret the image. Figure 1.1 illustrates the main components of a commonly used type of figure—the line graph.

Organization of the Book

There are so many types and styles of figures that it would be next to impossible to present them all in a single book. We have thus limited the scope of this book to examples of the more common figures found in the psychology literature.

In designing this book we have, to a certain extent, used APA's categorization of figures: Everything that is not text or a table or an exhibit is considered to be a figure. We present nine different kinds of

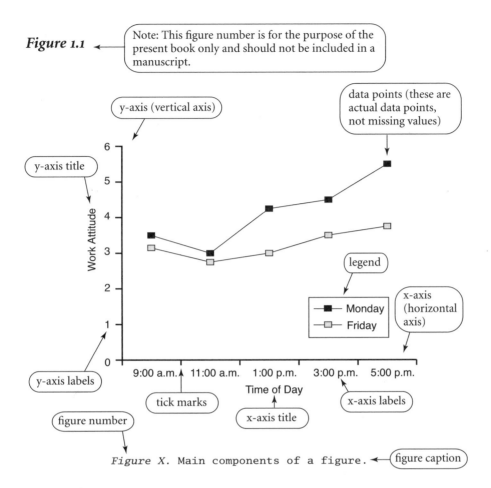

Figure 1.1

Note: This figure number is for the purpose of the present book only and should not be included in a manuscript.

Figure X. Main components of a figure.

figures: bar graphs, line graphs, plots, drawings, combination graphs (which combine graphs or incorporate drawings or photographs), pie graphs, miscellaneous graphs (dendrograms and stem-and-leaf plots), charts, and photographs. Each is used to present different kinds of information. Each type of figure is described in a separate chapter. In addition, the last two chapters provide guidelines for preparing poster presentations for conferences and slides and overheads for presentations.

Unlike our book on tables, the chapters in the present book are not organized according to type of analysis. Figures are not always essential, so we did not wish to mislead readers by organizing the book by statistics. Instead, we have organized the book by type of figure. Furthermore, some types of figures are so rarely used that we did not include them in this book. This does not mean that authors cannot use them in a manuscript; authors simply should follow as closely as possible APA guidelines and the checklists we provide.

The following is a description of the various parts of each chapter.

Type of Figure

Subtype

What Type of Data Is Presented?

The first section of each chapter explains the type of data or information presented in the chapter (e.g., change in scores over time or over a number of trials).

Example

In the example section, we briefly describe a fictional study. We have included examples from different areas of psychology, such as clinical psychology, cognitive psychology, developmental psychology, educational psychology, industrial/organizational psychology, neuroscience, and social psychology. If the results of a statistical procedure (e.g., multidimensional scaling) or a specific type of data (e.g., event-related potentials) are presented, then we briefly describe that procedure or data. An exhibit, presented in a box following the description of the study, lists the variables to help the reader identify the key elements of the study.

Figures

The figures constructed for the fictional study constitute the bulk of each chapter. Text bubbles accompanying each figure enclose explanatory comments. More than one version of the same figure may be presented to show acceptable (or inadvisable) variations in figure elements. Each figure is identified by a figure number denoting both the number of the chapter in this book and the order of the figure within the chapter (e.g., Figure 3.6 is the sixth figure in chapter 3).

Figures illustrating sample figures (as opposed to figures illustrating sample posters and visual aids) have a second figure number and a figure caption, representative of what would actually appear in a manuscript. These figure captions begin with the words *Figure X,* with the *X* representing the appropriate figure number in a particular manuscript.

Checklist of Effective Elements

At the end of each chapter, we present checklists of elements that make a figure or presentation particularly useful and attention-getting and conform to APA guidelines. The checklist at the end of this first chapter is a general checklist that applies to all of the figures presented in this book. To make this general checklist easy to use, it is presented at the end of every chapter pertaining to figures. In addition, many chapters contain a more specific checklist that applies to the types of figures or visual presentations discussed in that chapter.

A Few Caveats

The figures presented in this book are intended to be used as models to assist researchers in designing their own figures. The example research studies on which they are based are greatly simplified; we do not claim that the example studies provide the best means of conducting a study or illustrate the best way to analyze data. This book is not a research methods book or a statistics book, and we have not presented theoretical explanations for the example studies because our focus is data presentation, not experimental design. In most instances, descriptive and inferential statistics have not been provided, as these should be presented in the text of the manuscript or within tables. We have not presented all of the information that should be presented when reporting results. Furthermore, some information presented in figures could instead be presented in text or in tables, depending on the preferences of the researcher.

Finally, all of the examples provided are fictional. Any likeness to actual studies is purely coincidental.

Guidelines for Preparing Figures

How the data are presented is crucial for comprehension. The author's or presenter's primary goal is always to ensure that the audience understands the research project. Otherwise, the impact of the research is compromised.

Most of the figures in this book were originally created using widely accessible programs such as Microsoft Word, Microsoft PowerPoint, and Microsoft Excel. Any software that the user feels comfortable with and that produces graphics with clearly distinguishable lines, shapes, shades, and contrasts is acceptable. Naturally, no matter how superb the program is, the final result will depend on the type of printer used; dot-matrix printers produce poorer quality figures than laser or inkjet printers. Many journal and book publishers have very specific requirements about figure format, and authors are expected to follow them.

Figures 1.2–1.4 illustrate how to submit a figure for publication.

General Guidelines for Figures

The following guidelines for preparing figures are relevant for any manuscript. Therefore, they should be followed in preparing figures for theses, manuscripts not to be published, and manuscripts submitted to journals and books not requiring APA format, as well as for manuscripts submitted to journals or books requiring APA format.

- The figure must be relevant to the manuscript and play a key role in the section in which it is mentioned (e.g., Introduction, Method, Results, Discussion).
- The figure image should be as simple as possible; only essential information should be included.
- Labels should be as concise as possible.
- Text fonts should be consistent within the figure and consistent across all figures presented in a single manuscript.
- The use of color should be avoided; most journals, books, theses, and reports are printed in black and white. Color can, however, be used effectively in conference posters, slides, or overheads.
- The units of measurement should be specified within the figure.
- A figure should be understandable on its own. All information

Figure 1.2

When preparing figures for journal or book submissions, the Figure Caption page is placed at the end of the manuscript, followed by the figures, which begin on a separate page. The figures and captions are incorporated into the text later in the publication process. In material not being submitted for publication (e.g., a thesis or report), authors may insert each figure and its corresponding caption into the manuscript in the first available space after the figure is first mentioned in the text. Departmental guidelines should be followed.

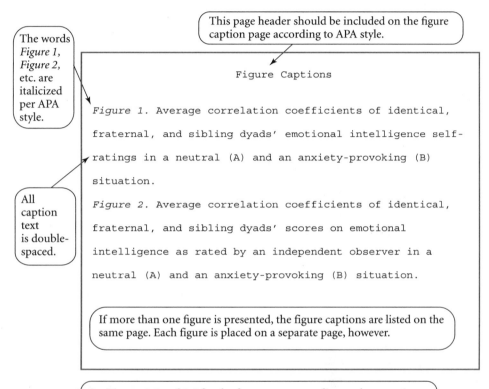

This page header should be included on the figure caption page according to APA style.

The words *Figure 1*, *Figure 2*, etc. are italicized per APA style.

All caption text is double-spaced.

Figure Captions

Figure 1. Average correlation coefficients of identical, fraternal, and sibling dyads' emotional intelligence self-ratings in a neutral (A) and an anxiety-provoking (B) situation.

Figure 2. Average correlation coefficients of identical, fraternal, and sibling dyads' scores on emotional intelligence as rated by an independent observer in a neutral (A) and an anxiety-provoking (B) situation.

If more than one figure is presented, the figure captions are listed on the same page. Each figure is placed on a separate page, however.

See Figures 1.3 and 1.4 for the figures corresponding to these captions.

needed to interpret the figure (e.g., abbreviations, definitions) should be included in the caption. Very little explanation should be required in the text.

Figure 1.3

This is Figure 1 of a sample manuscript.

A page on which a figure is presented should not include a page header. Each figure should be identified in handwriting on the top right edge of the front of the figure or on the back if there is not enough room on the front.

Figure 1 would be handwritten on the manuscript in this area, space permitting.

A

Neutral Situation

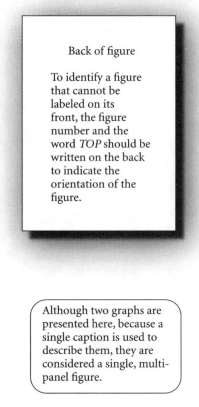

Back of figure

To identify a figure that cannot be labeled on its front, the figure number and the word *TOP* should be written on the back to indicate the orientation of the figure.

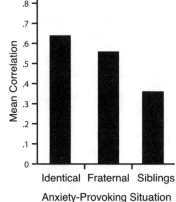

B

Anxiety-Provoking Situation

Although two graphs are presented here, because a single caption is used to describe them, they are considered a single, multi-panel figure.

Figure 1.4

This is Figure 2 of a sample manuscript.

Figure 2 would be handwritten on the manuscript in this area, space permitting.

If a single figure requires more than one panel, a capital letter (e.g., A, B) is placed on the top left corner of each panel. This letter should be 14 points.

Note that Figures 1 and 2 are the same size and use the same scale to permit easy comparisons.

Guidelines for Figures That Follow APA Style

In addition to the general guidelines, several other considerations are relevant when the figure is to be submitted to a journal requiring APA format:

- Authors should read and follow the guidelines for figure preparation in the APA *Publication Manual.*
- Shadings should be easily distinguishable from one another and able to be clearly reduced and reproduced.
- Most figures need to be reduced to fit the journal or book's format (e.g., column width). All elements of the figure (e.g., patterns, type size) must still be clear when reduced to fit the journal's or book's measurements. (This can be estimated by reducing the image using a photocopier.)
- Text within the figure should be in a sans serif font (letters with no cross bars at their tips, usually Helvetica or Arial.
- The font sizes within the figure should not differ from one another by more than 4 points.
- Labels should be parallel to their respective axes.

Guidelines for Figure Legends

If a legend is required, usually to define line styles, data point symbols, or shading used to differentiate data sets, a few guidelines need to be followed:

- Incorporate the legend into the body of the figure image (e.g., if any axes are present, place the legend within their boundaries wherever there is white space). If the legend is located outside the body of the image, thus enlarging its dimensions, the figure will need to be reduced more to fit the space available. Following this guideline will ensure that the figure is reduced as little as possible and better retains its clarity and legibility.
- Use the same sans serif font as in the rest of the figure.
- Clearly identify and define each element that needs explanation (e.g., line styles, data point symbols, and shading variants).

Guidelines for Figure Captions

Figure captions consist of a figure number (e.g., Figure 1, Figure 3) and a short description of the figure. The following guidelines should be followed in preparing figure captions:

- Briefly describe the figure.
- Explain any abbreviations used within the figure that are not identified in the legend of the figure.
- If error bars are included in the figure, describe what they mean.
- Include sample sizes, statistics used, and probability levels as necessary.
- Type figure captions in the same font as that used in the text of the manuscript. This should be a serif font (i.e., the letters contain crossbars at their tips) such as Times New Roman or `Courier`.
- Type the figure caption page double-spaced.

Guidelines for Placement of Figures and Captions

Use the following guidelines when preparing a figure for publication using APA guidelines:

- Place the image on one page and the caption on a page of its own (along with a page header—e.g., "Figure Captions"). See Figure 1.2 for a sample Figure Captions page that would accompany Figures 1.3 and 1.4.
- If there is more than one figure, place each figure on a separate page, and place the captions one after the other on the captions page (more pages are used only if a single page cannot accommodate all of the captions).
- Position the caption page, followed by all figures, at the end of the manuscript (after the references, author notes, footnotes, and tables) to permit separate departments (e.g., typesetting, scanning) to reproduce the figure efficiently.
- When preparing a figure for a thesis or report, incorporate the figure and caption into the text of the manuscript as soon as possible after the figure has been mentioned in the text (follow guidelines specified by the department).

Checklist of Effective Elements for All Figures

- All text in figure uses the same style font (sans serif).
- Font sizes within a figure do not vary by more than 4 points.
- Text in the caption uses the same font as the text of the manuscript.
- The caption is typed double-spaced.
- Figure captions are descriptive (i.e., they describe the variables of interest and other important information, such as what abbreviations mean).
- Figure captions are listed on a separate page.
- Lines are thick enough to be clear after reduction.
- Similar figures within the same manuscript have a similar appearance.
- Figures are referred to in the text using the figure number.

Conclusion

Our overall goal in writing this book was to help people present their findings in the most effective way. We hope that by presenting numerous examples, explanatory bubbles, and quick-reference checklists, we will have saved readers some time in creating their figures. Most important, we hope that readers can use elements of the sample figures and visuals in the book to enhance their own work. The success of this book will be defined by its usefulness.

CHAPTER 2

Bar Graphs

What Type of Data Is Presented?

Bar graphs (sometimes referred to as "column graphs") are useful in presenting or comparing differences between groups. Sometimes they are used to show how groups differ over time. Although a minimum of two bars is required, it is best to use this type of figure when four or more bars are to be presented.

Example 2.1

A group of researchers wished to examine the hand gesturing style of men and women. Participants were asked to tell a joke while they were being videotaped for 5 min. The number of large gestures, small gestures, single-hand gestures, and two-hand gestures were counted by three independent judges. Interrater reliability was high enough to average the three judges' total scores (see Figures 2.1–2.10).

Exhibit 2.1

Independent Variable
1. Gender (male, female)

Dependent Variables
1. Number of large hand gestures
2. Number of small hand gestures
3. Number of one-hand gestures
4. Number of two-hand gestures

Figure 2.1

The value of the dependent variable is most frequently placed on the y-axis (vertical axis).

The y-axis to x-axis length ratio should be appropriate (e.g., the y-axis should be from two thirds to three quarters the length of the x-axis).

The top of each bar indicates the value for a particular group (e.g., women presented an average of 6.5 large hand gestures).

The independent variable is most often placed on the x-axis (horizontal axis).

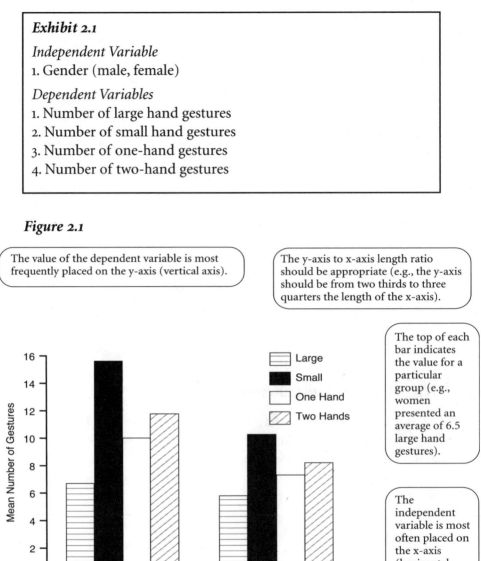

Figure X. Average number of times different types of hand gestures were used by women (*n* = 20) and men (*n* = 20) when telling a joke over a 5-min period.

Although differences between the patterns used to identify the bars may be observable on the computer monitor, when printed they may be indistinguishable. The appearance of the shading can best be verified by checking a laser printout.

Color can be used instead of shading for overheads, multimedia, or poster presentations to differentiate the bars. Most books and journals do not print color.

Figure 2.2

In this version of the figure, the numerical values for the dependent variable are provided above the top of each bar.

The legend should be placed within the boundaries of the axes so that the figure requires as little reduction as possible.

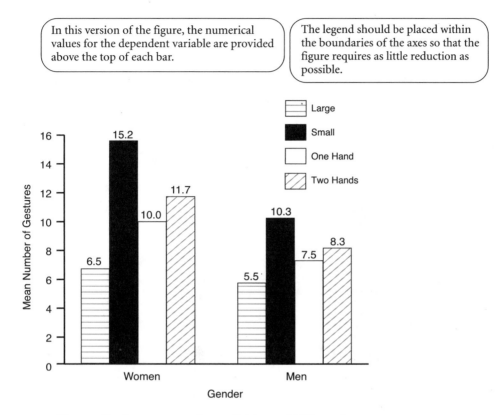

Figure X. Average number of times different types of hand gestures were used by women ($n = 20$) and men ($n = 20$) when telling a joke over a 5-min period.

The larger space between the *Women* and *Men* bars and the shorter space on either end of the x-axis help readers visually group the bars.

Little or no space should separate bars grouped within one level of the independent variable (e.g., the four bars within *Women*). Large spaces would make the graph not only larger but more difficult to read.

Figure 2.3

Grid lines are provided here, which can make the y-axis values easier to read, especially in figures that are wider than this one (i.e., figures with a very long x-axis).

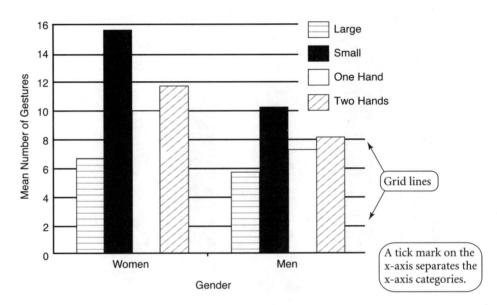

Grid lines

A tick mark on the x-axis separates the x-axis categories.

Figure X. Average number of times different types of hand gestures were used by women (*n* = 20) and men (*n* = 20) when telling a joke over a 5-min period.

Figure 2.4

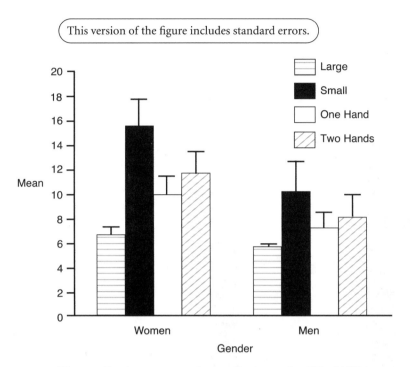

Figure X. Average number of times (± *SE*) different types of hand gestures were used by women (*n* = 20) and men (*n* = 20) when telling a joke over a 5-min period.

When possible, all axis labels should be parallel to the axes. However, on occasion, it may be necessary to present the x-axis labels perpendicular to the x-axis (see Figure 2.17). If the y-axis is no longer than 10 characters, it is acceptable to present the label perpendicular to the y-axis, as in the example above.

The figure caption identifies the error bars as standard error bars.

Figure 2.5

When double-sided error bars are used, they should be clearly observable on both ends for each of the bars. (They may not be apparent when very dark shading is used.)

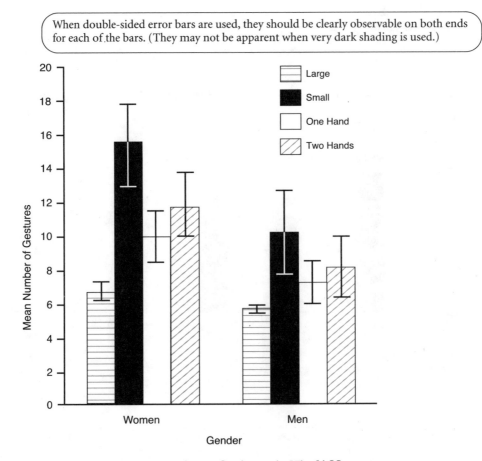

Figure X. Average number of times (±*SE*) different types of hand gestures were used by women (*n* = 20) and men (*n* = 20) when telling a joke over a 5-min period.

The caption specifies the sample size and identifies the error bars as standard error bars.

Figure 2.6

The bars within the same category are slightly separated from one another to help readers distinguish one bar from another. These spaces should be kept small, however, as large spaces would make the graph more difficult to read. Large spaces should be used only to distinguish different levels of an independent variable (e.g., *Women* and *Men*).

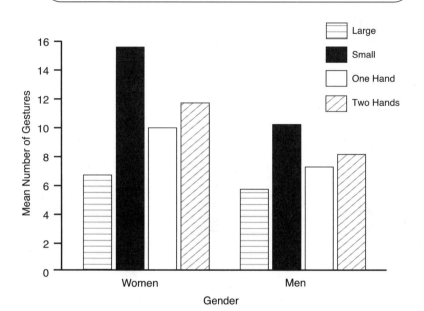

Figure X. Average number of times different types of hand gestures were used by women (*n* = 20) and men (*n* = 20) when telling a joke over a 5-min period.

Figure 2.7

The bars overlap in this version of the figure, particularly useful when there are many bars to present and the researcher wishes to save some space. Alternatively, skinnier bars could be used.

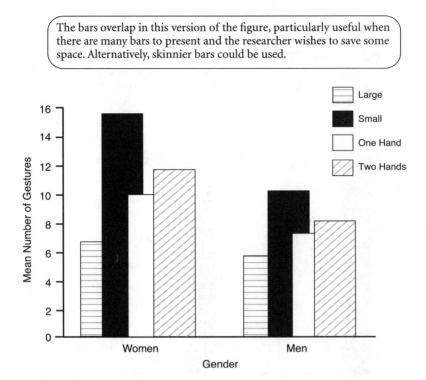

Figure X. Average number of times different hand gestures were used by women (*n* = 20) and men (*n* = 20) when telling a joke over a 5-min period.

Figure 2.8

This graph is sometimes referred to as a *stacked bar graph*. It permits the reader to make comparisons between overall frequencies but makes comparisons between bars more difficult.

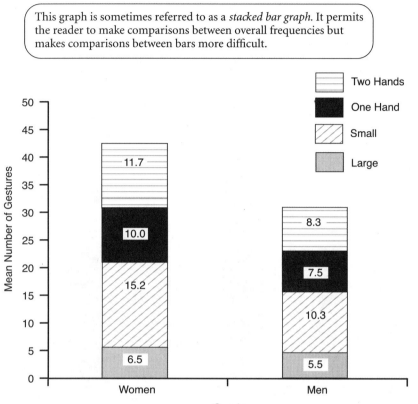

Figure X. Average number of times different hand gestures were used by women (*n* = 20) and men (*n* = 20) when telling a joke over a 5-min period.

The y-axis permits the reader to determine the mean totals for each bar as well as compare the individual means with the total mean. Because it is more difficult to estimate the values of the stacked bars, exact values should be provided within the bars.

Figure 2.9

Three-dimensional graphs may appear sophisticated, but they are considerably more difficult to read. It is best to keep graphs simple and avoid special effects that are visually distracting.

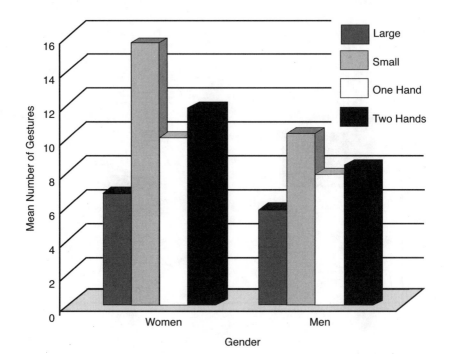

Figure X. Average number of times different types of hand gestures were used by women (*n* = 20) and men (*n* = 20) when telling a joke over a 5-min period.

Figure 2.10

> If the bar graph is getting too tall and all of the results are greater than 0, the y-axis may start at a value other than 0. The two diagonal lines on the y-axis alert the reader that the y-axis does not start at 0. Differences between groups may appear exaggerated when a y-axis break is introduced.

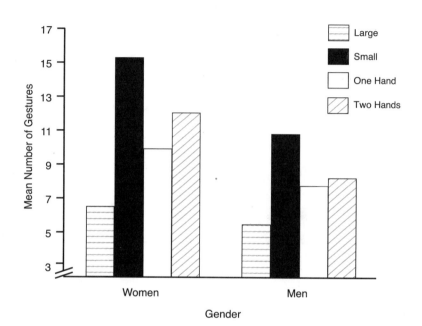

Figure X. Average number of times different types of hand gestures were used by women (*n* = 20) and men (*n* = 20) when telling a joke over a 5-min period.

Example 2.2

The same researchers wished to compare the hand gesturing styles of 20-year-old and 60-year-old men and women while telling a joke. Participants were given a script to memorize and asked to tell the story to another person while being videotaped. (The other person was the experimenters' accomplice, who was asked to react in a similar manner for all of the participants.) The number of large and small gestures were counted by two independent judges and averaged (interrater reliability indicated that averaging their scores was warranted). Figure 2.11 presents the results.

Figure 2.11

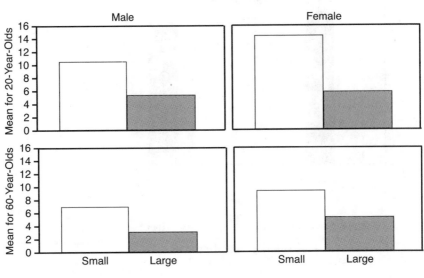

Figure X. The small and large hand gestures of 20-year-old and 60-year-old men and women when telling a joke.

Four graphs were created and placed together in a single figure.

Example 2.3

Two researchers wished to determine the extent to which hand gestures in early life match hand gestures later in life. One hundred and fifty 5-year-old children were classified into one of two groups: (a) many hand gestures present or (b) few hand gestures present. Fifteen years later these individuals were asked to allow a close friend to complete a paper-and-pencil measure to assess the extent to which they used a variety of hand gestures. The 20-year-olds were rated on the extent to which they used inclusive (draws other people into a conversation), exclusive (excludes other people from a conversation), relevant, and irrelevant hand gestures. Figures 2.12 and 2.13 present the results.

Exhibit 2.3

Independent Variable

1. Age (5 years old, 20 years old)

Dependent Variables

1. Hand gestures at age 5 (many, few)
2. Hand gestures at age 20 (inclusive, exclusive, relevant, irrelevant)

Figure 2.12

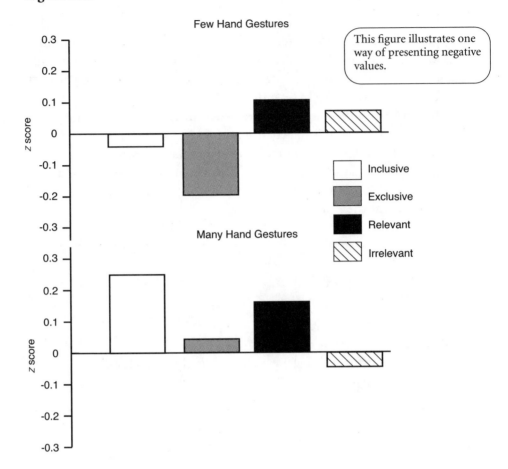

This figure illustrates one way of presenting negative values.

Figure X. Age 5 hand gesture behavior (few or many gestures) and the same participants' scores at age 20 on a hand gesture survey (inclusive, exclusive, relevant, irrelevant) as rated by a close peer. The figure shows z scores ($M = 0$, $SD = 1$) standardized on the full sample.

Figure 2.13

Here the bar graphs are presented somewhat differently from the previous figure. The axes have been switched; the dependent variable is on the x-axis rather than on the y-axis. This format is not frequently used because it is preferable to put the dependent variable on the y-axis.

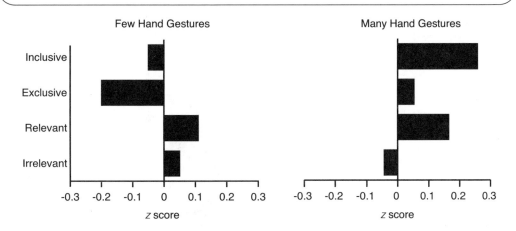

Figure X. Age 5 hand gesture behavior (few or many gestures) and the same participants' scores at age 20 on a hand gesture survey (inclusive, exclusive, relevant, irrelevant) as rated by a close peer. The figure shows z scores ($M = 0$, $SD = 1$) standardized on the full sample.

Example 2.4

A researcher sought to determine whether a performance goal-oriented training program, a learning goal-oriented training program, or a subject-based goal-oriented training program was better than the traditional training program used at a college to teach young adults about first aid. Individuals were placed in one of the four experimental conditions. Their results on a written test were then compared in Figures 2.14–2.16.

Exhibit 2.4

Independent Variable
1. Type of training program (traditional, performance, learning, subject-based)

Dependent Variable
1. Score on a written test

Figure 2.14

An asterisk can be used in bar graphs to indicate significance levels. The asterisk presented over the performance condition indicates that post hoc differences were found between that condition and each of the other groups. No intergroup differences were found for the traditional, learning, and subject groups.

Figure X. Mean test scores for participants in the traditional (*n* = 22), performance (*n* = 21), learning (*n* = 17), and subject-based (*n* = 19) goal-oriented groups.
*p < .01.

The asterisk in the figure must be described in the figure caption.

Figure 2.15

Just as the two diagonal lines crossing the y-axis indicate that the starting point is not 0, an ellipsis on the y-axis indicates that the intervening values have been left out. This is done when one or more of the bars is too high or long in comparison with the other bars in the same graph.

Figure X. Mean test scores for participants in the traditional (*n* = 22), performance (*n* = 21), learning (*n* = 17), and subject-based (*n* = 19) goal-oriented groups.

Figure 2.16

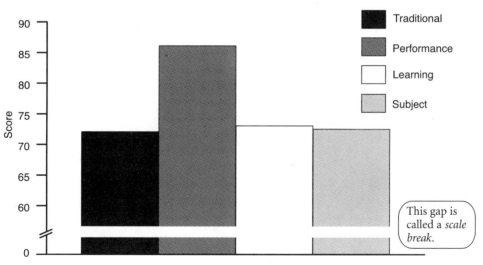

This gap is called a *scale break*.

Figure X. Mean test scores for participants in the traditional (*n* = 22), performance (*n* = 21), learning (*n* = 17), and subject-based (*n* = 19) goal-oriented groups.

If the researcher wishes to start the y-axis at 0 and introduce a scale break somewhere along the y-axis, two diagonal lines can be inserted higher up on the y-axis. A space (the scale break) should be inserted across the bars at a height that is level with the two lines on the y-axis.

Example 2.5

A researcher wished to determine whether individuals in various traditional professions felt fulfilled and had a sense of what the meaning of life is. He obtained nominal lists of accountants, administrative assistants, garment workers, cooks, dentists, general practitioners, graduate students, high-level managers, low-level managers, maintenance (cleaning) engineers, mechanics, ministers/priests/rabbis, nurses, professors, sales clerks, servers (waiters/waitresses), and taxi drivers. He sent each person on his list a fulfillment/meaning of life survey. He obtained a 30% response rate and compared the responses by trade, as shown in Figure 2.17.

Exhibit 2.5

Independent Variable
1. Trade (accountant, administrative assistant, garment worker, cook, dentist, general practitioner, graduate student, high-level manager, low-level manager, maintenance engineer, mechanic, minister/priest/rabbi, nurse, professor, sales clerk, server, taxi driver)

Dependent Variable
1. Fulfillment/meaning of life score

Figure 2.17

Because of the large number of bars, a second y-axis has been included on the right of this graph to make it easier to estimate the values of the bars on the right. (Including the exact values on or above the bars may require a font size that is too small.) In addition, the x-axis labels have been placed perpendicular to the axis so they will fit.

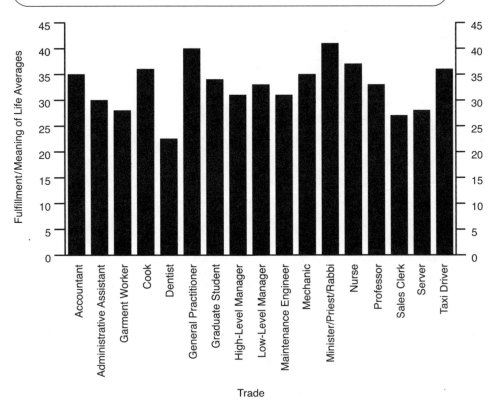

Figure X. Average scores on the fulfillment/meaning of life scale for the 17 professions studied.

Abbreviations (e.g., letter or number designations) for the trades could be used on the x-axis, but they would require explanation in the figure caption. This should be done only when necessary; looking back and forth from the figure to the caption to determine what each bar represents is an inconvenience for readers.

Because there is only one bar for each trade, it is not necessary to shade the bars differently.

Example 2.6

Three researchers were studying whether men's and women's feelings of fulfillment were the same at various ages. The researchers
asked men and women of various age groups to complete a fulfill-
ment/meaning of life survey. The age groups they studied were
20–29, 30–39, 40–49, 50–59, 60–69, and 70–79. They presented their
results in Figure 2.18.

Exhibit 2.6

Independent Variables
1. Gender (female, male)
2. Age category (20–29, 30–39, 40–49, 50–59, 60–69, 70–79)

Dependent Variable
1. Fulfillment/meaning of life score

Figure 2.18

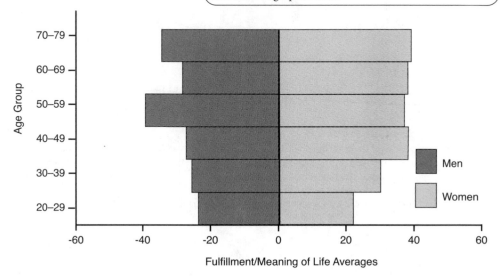

The dependent variable is on the x-axis and not on the y-axis in this example.

This is an example of an upside-down pyramid graph. It is not frequently used because it is preferable to put the dependent variable on the y-axis rather than on the x-axis. Nevertheless, comparisons are easy to make when this form of graph is used.

Figure X. Average fulfillment/meaning of life scores for men and
women in various age ranges.

Checklist of Effective Elements for All Figures

- All text in figure uses the same style font (sans serif).
- Font sizes within a figure do not vary by more than 4 points.
- Text in the caption uses the same font as the text of the manuscript.
- The caption is typed double-spaced.
- Figure captions are descriptive (i.e., they describe the variables of interest and other important information, such as what abbreviations mean).
- Figure captions are listed on a separate page.
- Lines are thick enough to be clear after reduction.
- Similar figures within the same manuscript have a similar appearance.
- Figures are referred to in the text using the figure number.

Checklist of Effective Elements for Bar Graphs

- In axis labels and titles, the first letter of the first word and all major words are capitalized.
- In legends, the first letter of the first word and all major words are capitalized.
- The dependent variable is on the vertical (y) axis (unless there is a reason to put it on the x-axis).
- The independent variable is on the horizontal (x) axis (unless there is a reason to put it on the y-axis).
- The y-axis/x-axis length ratio is appropriate (usually, the y-axis should be two thirds to three quarters the length of the x-axis).
- Axes are clearly labeled.
- Axis labels are parallel to the axes, if possible.
- Positive values on the x-axis increase to the right, whereas those on the y-axis increase up.
- Negative values on the x-axis increase to the left, whereas those on the y-axis increase down.
- The highest values on the x-axis and y-axis scales are larger than the highest data values (i.e., the x- and y-axes are longer than the area covered by the largest data values).
- Bars representing different independent variables within the graph can be clearly differentiated from one another.
- Bars are of the same width.

- Spaces used to separate bars are of the same width.
- The legend is presented within the image's boundaries.
- Tick marks are long enough and thick enough to be visible without distracting.

CHAPTER 3

Line Graphs

What Type of Data Is Presented?

A line graph is used to present a change in one or more dependent variables as a function of an independent variable. It is particularly useful in demonstrating a trend or an interaction. Types of data effectively presented using a line graph include average changes in scores for the dependent variable over time, trials, or some other independent variable and average correlations over trials or time.

A line graph figure must have at least 3 data points; it is much more common to see 4 points (particularly to present interaction effects) or even up to 10 points in a single-line graph. The APA *Publication Manual* recommends using no more than four lines (curves) per graph.

Example 3.1

A senior undergraduate student wrote 30 items that she hoped would form a new measure of naïveté. As part of the validation study, she conducted a principal-components analysis to determine the factor structure of the measure. In her thesis she presented a *scree plot* (which shows the proportion of variance that is accounted for by the individual factors) to illustrate the number of factors in her measure (Figure 3.1).

Exhibit 3.1

Variable
1. Thirty items of the naïveté questionnaire

Figure 3.1

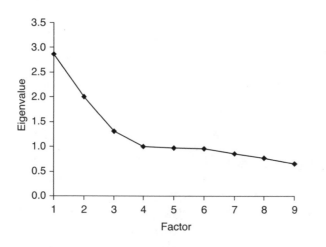

Figure X. Scree plot of the measure of naïveté.

Example 3.2

A student was interested in learning whether the topic of industrial/organizational (I/O) psychology was perceived by graduate students to be covered in introductory psychology textbooks more now than in the past. She asked graduate students to estimate the number of pages devoted to I/O psychology in the typical introductory psychology textbooks published between 1950 and 2000. She presented the results in a line graph (see Figures 3.2–3.5).

Exhibit 3.2

Independent Variable

1. Year introductory psychology textbook was published (1950 to 2000)

Dependent Variable

1. Estimates of the number of pages devoted to I/O psychology in introductory psychology textbooks each year

Figure 3.2

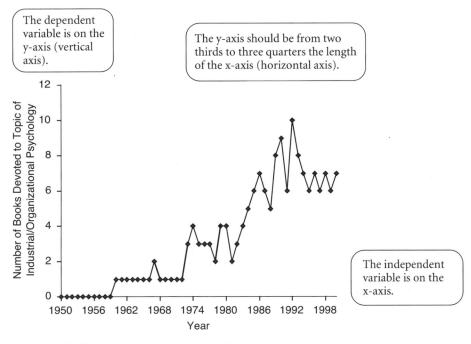

Figure X. Mean estimates by graduate students of the number of pages devoted to industrial/ organizational psychology in introductory psychology textbooks published between 1950 and 2000.

Figure 3.3

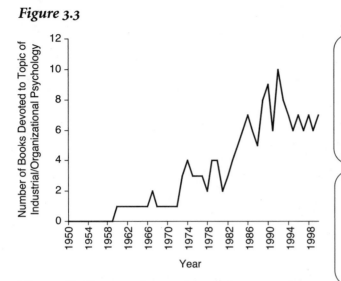

Data points should be highlighted using a small character such as a square or a circle to help the reader read the graph more accurately. Note how in this figure the values for years not labeled on the x-axis are more difficult to discern than they are in Figure 3.2.

Although it is preferable to present all axis labels parallel to the axes, it may be necessary to present numerous x-axis labels angled or perpendicular to the x-axis. Y-axis labels no longer than 10 characters may also be perpendicular.

Figure X. Mean estimates by graduate students of the number of pages devoted to industrial/ organizational psychology in introductory psychology textbooks published between 1950 and 2000.

Figure 3.4

In this figure, some of the data points are labeled to facilitate reading the graph.

The font sizes used within a figure should not differ by more than 4 points. (In this figure, everything is 8 points, except for the axis titles, which are 10 points—a 2-point difference.)

Figure X. Mean estimates by graduate students of the number of pages devoted to industrial/organizational psychology in introductory psychology textbooks published between 1950 and 2000.

Figure 3.5

Horizontal grid lines are included to facilitate reading the values on the y-axis. If grid lines are too close together, they can clutter the figure.

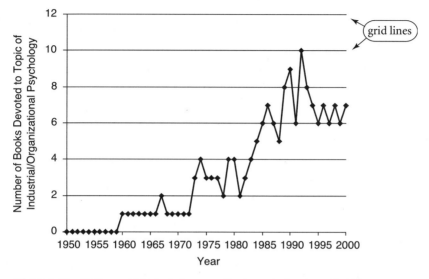

Figure X. Mean estimates by graduate students of the number of pages devoted to industrial/organizational psychology in introductory psychology textbooks published between 1950 and 2000.

Example 3.3

In addition to the estimated number of pages in introductory psychology textbooks that covered topics in I/O psychology, the Example 3.2 student wished to determine the extent to which paranormal psychology was covered in these same books. The same participants were asked to estimate the extent to which their introductory psychology books covered the topic of paranormal psychology. The results are presented in Figure 3.6.

Exhibit 3.3

Independent Variable

1. Year introductory psychology textbook was published (1950 to 2000)

Dependent Variables

1. Estimates of the number of pages devoted to I/O psychology in introductory psychology textbooks each year
2. Estimates of the number of pages devoted to paranormal psychology in introductory psychology textbooks each year

Figure 3.6

Axis labels should be concise enough to fit on one line.

When there are two or more lines, changing the line style and data point symbols can make the graph easier to read, especially when the lines overlap or cross.

The legend has been placed within the boundaries of the axes.

Simple symbols (squares, circles) are used. Distracting symbols such as stars or happy faces should be avoided.

Figure X. Mean estimates of the number of pages devoted to industrial/organizational psychology and paranormal psychology in introductory psychology textbooks published between 1950 and 2000.

Although differences among symbols and lines may be clear on the computer monitor, they may not be visible in printed form. The appearance can best be verified by making a black-and-white laser printout.

Color can be used to differentiate lines and symbols for overheads, multimedia, or poster presentations (see chapters 11 and 12). However, most books and journals do not print color, especially for simple line art.

Example 3.4

A researcher wished to determine the effectiveness of a meditation technique in reducing a nervous eye-blinking tic. Two groups of individuals participated: One group had developed an eye-blinking tic within the past year and the other had had the tic for 5 or more years. The researcher first obtained a series of baseline measures by filming each participant for an hour at four separate sessions and counting the number of eye-blinking tics. The average number of eye-blinking tics per 5 min was calculated for each of the four sessions. Then participants were taught to use a deep breathing and relaxation meditation technique. Participants used the technique for 15 min a day for 1 week and then stopped using the technique for a week. This cycle was maintained for 8 weeks, with measures of eye-blinking tics taken three times each week (for a total of 4 baseline measures and 24 experimental measures). Figures 3.7–3.9 illustrate the results.

Exhibit 3.4

Independent Variables

1. Session—measurement (via 1 hr of filming) of eye-blinking tic three times per week during use or nonuse of a deep breathing and relaxation meditation technique
2. Length of time an eye-blinking tic was present (up to 1 year, over 5 years)

Dependent Variable

1. Average number of eye-blinking tics in a 5-min period

Figure 3.7

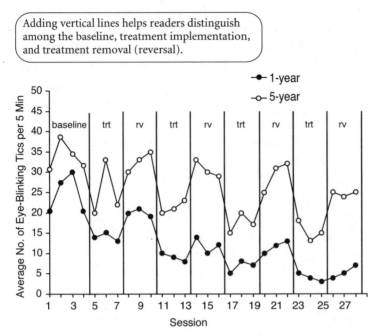

Adding vertical lines helps readers distinguish among the baseline, treatment implementation, and treatment removal (reversal).

Figure X. Average number of eye-blinking tics for participants with a tic problem for up to 1 year (*n* = 24) and for participants with a tic problem for a minimum of 5 years (*n* = 18). trt = treatment; rv = reversal.

The labels on the x-axis are directly under, rather than between, the tick marks to help readers interpret the values.

The figure caption identifies sample sizes and defines abbreviations.

Figure 3.8

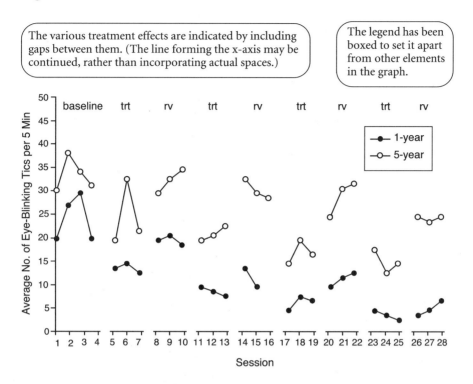

The various treatment effects are indicated by including gaps between them. (The line forming the x-axis may be continued, rather than incorporating actual spaces.)

The legend has been boxed to set it apart from other elements in the graph.

Figure X. Average number of eye-blinking tics for participants with this problem for up to 1 year (*n* = 24) and for participants with this problem for a minimum of 5 years (*n* = 18). trt = treatment; rv = reversal.

Figure 3.9

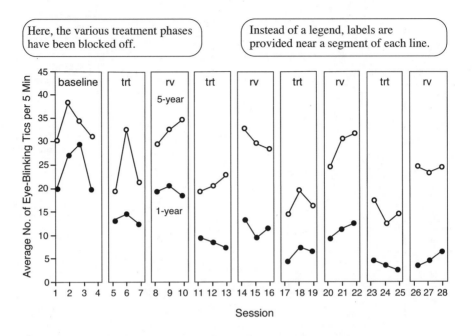

Figure X. Average number of eye-blinking tics for participants with a tic problem for up to 1 year (*n* = 24) and for participants with a tic problem for a minimum of 5 years (*n* = 18). trt = treatment; rv = reversal.

Example 3.5

The Example 3.4 researcher wished to determine whether participants in the eye-blinking tic study would continue to demonstrate lower levels of tics after a 6-month delay. He obtained baseline measures again and measures after two treatments and one reversal. To compare the results with the earlier study, he could choose to include all of the results in a single line graph (Figure 3.10) or in two graphs within one figure (Figure 3.11).

Exhibit 3.5

Independent Variables

1. Session—measurement (via 1 hr of filming) of eye-blinking tic three times per week following use or nonuse of a deep breathing and relaxation meditation technique
2. Length of time an eye-blinking tic was present (up to 1 year, over 5 years)

Dependent Variable

1. Average number of eye-blinking tics in a 5-min period

Figure 3.10

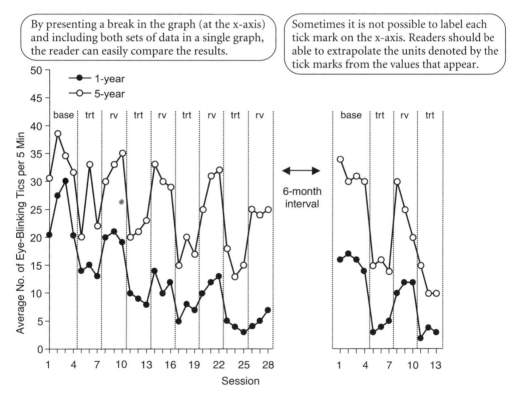

By presenting a break in the graph (at the x-axis) and including both sets of data in a single graph, the reader can easily compare the results.

Sometimes it is not possible to label each tick mark on the x-axis. Readers should be able to extrapolate the units denoted by the tick marks from the values that appear.

Figure X. Average number of eye-blinking tics for participants with a tic problem for up to 1 year ($n = 24$) and for participants with a tic problem for a minimum of 5 years ($n = 18$). Eye-blinking tics were counted at baseline and over an 8-week period of alternating introduction and reversal of the treatment. After 6 months, baseline measures and treatment and reversal were implemented again ($n = 19$ for the 1-year sample, $n = 10$ for the 5-year sample). base = baseline; trt = treatment; rv = reversal.

Figure 3.11

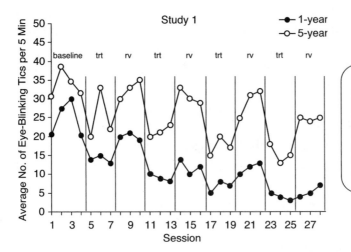

The two graphs are presented separately, but in a single figure. Each graph has an explanatory subtitle above it that is referred to in the caption.

Figure X. Average number of eye-blinking tics for participants with a tic problem for up to 1 year ($n = 24$) and for participants with a tic problem for a minimum of 5 years ($n = 18$). In Study 1, eye-blinking tics were counted at baseline and over an 8-week period of alternating introduction and reversal of the treatment. After 6 months, baseline measures and treatment and reversal were implemented again for Study 2 ($n = 19$ for the 1-year sample, $n = 10$ for the 5-year sample). trt = treatment; rv = reversal.

Example 3.6

The Example 3.4 researcher sought to determine the effectiveness of an exercise program on the reduction of an eye-blinking tic. As in Example 3.4, two groups of individuals participated: One group had developed an eye-blinking tic within the past year, and the other had had the tic for 5 or more years. The researcher first obtained three baseline measures of the number of eye-blinking tics and calculated the average number of eye tics per 5 min for each of the three measures. The individuals then participated in a 1-hr aerobics class every 3 days and refrained from extensive physical activity at other times. Measures of eye-blinking tics were taken every day. A total of six aerobics classes were given. Figures 3.12–3.15 illustrate various ways the results could be displayed.

Exhibit 3.6

Independent Variables
1. Aerobics classes
2. The length of time an eye-blinking tic was present (1 year, over 5 years)

Dependent Variable
1. Average number of eye-blinking tics in a 5-min period

Figure 3.12

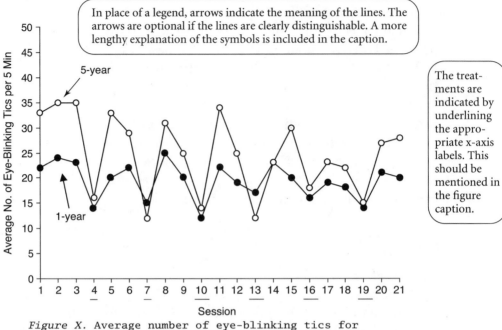

In place of a legend, arrows indicate the meaning of the lines. The arrows are optional if the lines are clearly distinguishable. A more lengthy explanation of the symbols is included in the caption.

The treatments are indicated by underlining the appropriate x-axis labels. This should be mentioned in the figure caption.

Figure X. Average number of eye-blinking tics for participants with a tic problem for up to 1 year (*n* = 17; black circles) and for participants with a tic problem for a minimum of 5 years (*n* = 15; white circles). Underlined x-axis labels denote measures taken immediately after an aerobics class.

Figure 3.13

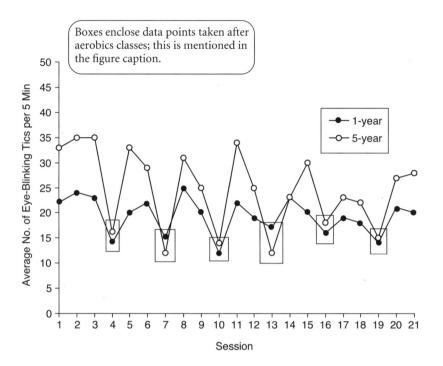

Boxes enclose data points taken after aerobics classes; this is mentioned in the figure caption.

Figure X. Average number of eye-blinking tics for participants with a tic problem for up to 1 year (*n* = 17) and for participants with a tic problem for a minimum of 5 years (*n* = 15). Boxes enclose measures taken immediately after an aerobics class.

Figure 3.14

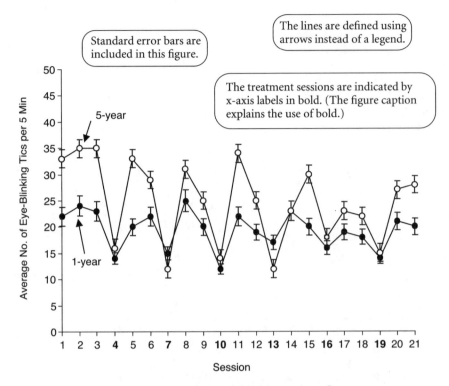

Standard error bars are included in this figure.

The lines are defined using arrows instead of a legend.

The treatment sessions are indicated by x-axis labels in bold. (The figure caption explains the use of bold.)

Figure X. Average number of eye-blinking tics for participants with a tic problem for up to 1 year (*n* = 17; black circles) and for participants with a tic problem for a minimum of 5 years (*n* = 15; white circles). Standard errors are also provided. Bold axis labels denote measures taken immediately after an aerobics class.

The standard error bars in the graph are identified as such in the caption.

Figure 3.15

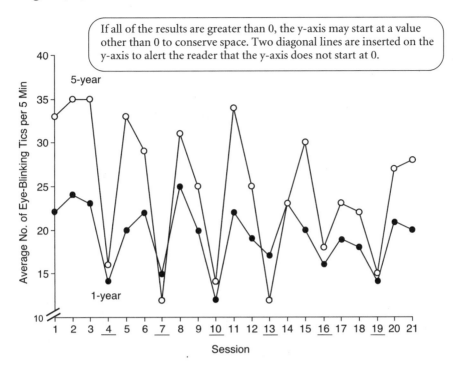

If all of the results are greater than 0, the y-axis may start at a value other than 0 to conserve space. Two diagonal lines are inserted on the y-axis to alert the reader that the y-axis does not start at 0.

Figure X. Average number of eye-blinking tics for participants with a tic problem for up to 1 year (*n* = 17; black circles) and for participants with a tic problem for a minimum of 5 years (*n* = 15; white circles). Standard errors are also provided. Underlined x-axis labels denote measures taken immediately after an aerobics class.

Example 3.7

Three researchers wished to examine the effects of stress and violent television on 8-year-old children. Stress was operationalized as the anticipation of an upcoming exam (high stress) or the absence of an upcoming exam (low stress). The violent television programs consisted of two animation shows shown on a cable network station on Saturday mornings (independent raters rated the two shows for violence prior to the commencement of the study). Children who participated did not have access to this cable network, and their parents permitted them to take part in the study.

The researchers developed a 2 x 2 experimental design whereby participants were placed in one of four conditions: (a) high stress and high TV violence, (b) low stress and high TV violence, (c) high stress and low TV violence, and (d) low stress and low TV violence. The researchers wished to determine whether there was an effect on children's aggressive behavior (children were filmed and their behavior coded by independent raters). Furthermore, the researchers wished to determine whether there was an interaction effect between the two independent variables. Figure 3.16 presents their results.

Exhibit 3.7

Independent Variables
1. Stress (high, low)
2. Violence (high, low)

Dependent Variable
1. Aggression

Figure 3.16

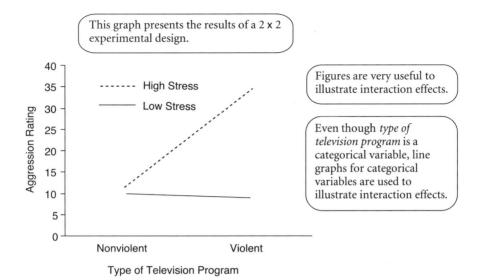

This graph presents the results of a 2 x 2 experimental design.

Figures are very useful to illustrate interaction effects.

Even though *type of television program* is a categorical variable, line graphs for categorical variables are used to illustrate interaction effects.

Figure X. Aggression level as a function of television violence and level of stress in a sample of 40 eight-year-old children, with 10 children per condition.

Example 3.8

The Example 3.7 researchers wished to determine whether there was a 2 x 3 x 2 (three-way) interaction effect among stress level, television violence, and sugar intake. Stress and violent programming were operationalized in a similar manner as in Example 3.7 except that an extra condition was added to the violent programming: a moderate violence condition. For the additional independent variable of sugar intake, children were given a drink of either (a) water, flavoring, and sugar or (b) water, flavoring, and artificial sweetener. Figures 3.17–3.20 depict different ways of presenting the results.

Exhibit 3.8

Independent Variables
1. Stress (low, high)
2. Violence (none, medium, high)
3. Sugar (none, high)

Dependent Variable
1. Aggression

Figure 3.17

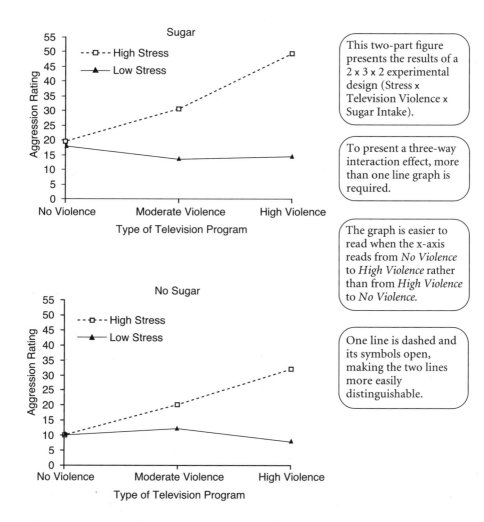

This two-part figure presents the results of a 2 x 3 x 2 experimental design (Stress x Television Violence x Sugar Intake).

To present a three-way interaction effect, more than one line graph is required.

The graph is easier to read when the x-axis reads from *No Violence* to *High Violence* rather than from *High Violence* to *No Violence*.

One line is dashed and its symbols open, making the two lines more easily distinguishable.

Figure X. Aggression in a sample of 120 children as a function of stress level, level of violence in a television program, and sugar intake.

Figure 3.18

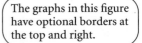

The graphs in this figure have optional borders at the top and right.

Figure X. Aggression in a sample of 120 children as a function of stress level, level of violence in a television program, and sugar intake.

Figure 3.19

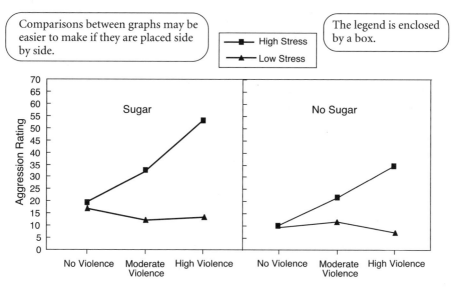

Comparisons between graphs may be easier to make if they are placed side by side.

The legend is enclosed by a box.

Type of Television Program

Figure X. Aggression in a sample of 120 children as a function of stress level, level of violence in a television program, and sugar intake.

The y-axis labels have not been repeated in the No Sugar graph to avoid clutter. Repeating the tick marks makes the values easier to estimate. Similarly, the graphs share one x-axis title, centered beneath them, to avoid unnecessary duplication.

Figure 3.20

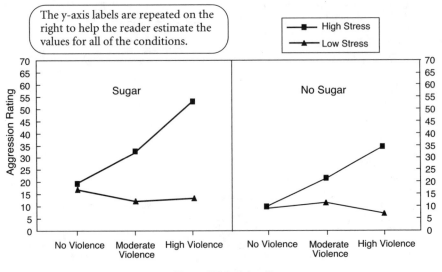

Figure X. Aggression in a sample of 120 children as a function of stress level, level of violence in a television program, and sugar intake.

Example 3.9

The Example 3.8 researchers wished to examine how moderate sugar intake level and moderate stress level would influence the level of aggression in children. There are still three independent variables, but now there are three levels of each independent variable; this is a 3 x 3 x 3 design. Results are presented in Figure 3.21.

Exhibit 3.9

Independent Variables
1. Stress (low, moderate, high)
2. Violence (none, medium, high)
3. Sugar (none, moderate, high)

Dependent Variable
1. Aggression

Figure 3.21

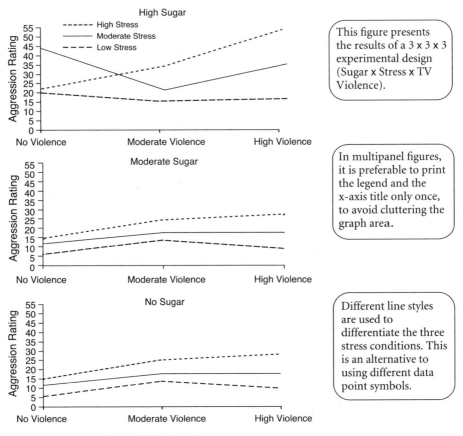

This figure presents the results of a 3 x 3 x 3 experimental design (Sugar x Stress x TV Violence).

In multipanel figures, it is preferable to print the legend and the x-axis title only once, to avoid cluttering the graph area.

Different line styles are used to differentiate the three stress conditions. This is an alternative to using different data point symbols.

Figure X. Aggression level for 8-year-olds as a function of stress level, level of violence in a television program, and level of sugar intake.

Example 3.10

A researcher was interested in the extent to which individuals with depression and individuals without depression are able to determine whether drawn faces are symmetrical or not. Each participant was tested individually in front of a computer screen that presented the various faces. The participant's task was to indicate using the keyboard whether the face presented was symmetrical or not. Each participant's reaction time and percentage of errors made were recorded by the computer, and Figures 3.22 and 3.23 present the results.

Exhibit 3.10

Independent Variable
1. Face symmetry (symmetrical, nonsymmetrical)

Dependent Variables
1. Reaction time in milliseconds
2. Percentage of errors made

Figure 3.22

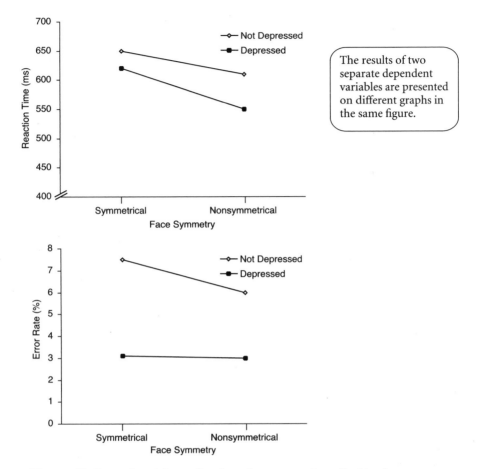

The results of two separate dependent variables are presented on different graphs in the same figure.

Figure X. Reaction times (top) and error rates (bottom) as a function of presence of depression and identification of facial symmetry.

Figure 3.23

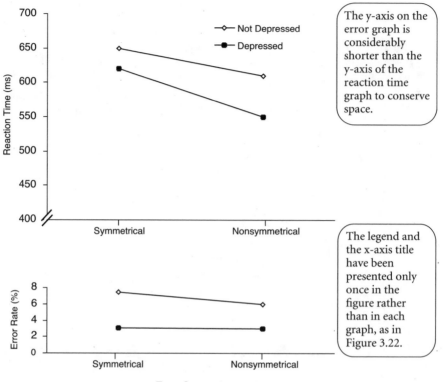

> The y-axis on the error graph is considerably shorter than the y-axis of the reaction time graph to conserve space.

> The legend and the x-axis title have been presented only once in the figure rather than in each graph, as in Figure 3.22.

Figure X. Reaction times (top) and error rates (bottom) as a function of presence of depression and identification of facial symmetry.

Example 3.11

A researcher working at a counseling center in a university wished to evaluate the center's test anxiety program. The anxiety program consisted of 2-hr weekly group instruction and counseling sessions for a maximum of 15 individuals for up to 4 weeks. The program was popular and usually had an extensive waiting list.

To conduct a program evaluation with an adequate sample size, the researcher decided to determine the progress of three different groups. Because the groups attended the program in consecutive months, the researcher obtained baseline measures over 2 weeks for the first group, 6 weeks for the second group, and 10 weeks for the third group. Each participant, once per week over the 4 weeks of the program, completed a test anxiety scale an hour before an exam and a generalized anxiety scale immediately after the exam. Also, participants completed the test anxiety and generalized anxiety scales 2 months after finishing the program. The researchers presented their results as shown in Figure 3.24.

Exhibit 3.11

Independent Variable
1. Test anxiety program

Dependent Variables
1. Generalized anxiety scale
2. Test anxiety scale

Figure 3.24

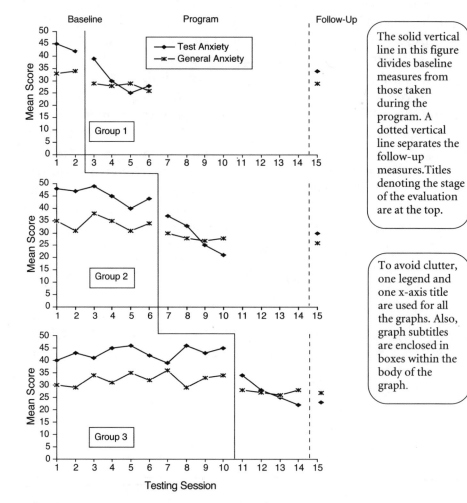

The solid vertical line in this figure divides baseline measures from those taken during the program. A dotted vertical line separates the follow-up measures. Titles denoting the stage of the evaluation are at the top.

To avoid clutter, one legend and one x-axis title are used for all the graphs. Also, graph subtitles are enclosed in boxes within the body of the graph.

Figure X. Average scores on test anxiety and general anxiety measures for three groups of participants taking a 4-week test anxiety course. Baseline, program intervention, and 1-month follow-up scores are presented for the three groups (Group 1, *n* = 15; Group 2, *n* = 13; Group 3, *n* = 14). Solid and dotted vertical lines separate the three stages of evaluation.

Example 3.12

A researcher wished to examine neurophysiological differences between bilingual and unilingual people when they listen to words pronounced incorrectly. Twenty individuals who spoke both English and French (bilinguals) and 20 individuals who spoke English only (unilinguals) participated in the study. Both groups of participants listened to English words that were pronounced correctly and English words that were pronounced incorrectly. Among the data collected were event-related potentials (ERPs), an average measure of voltage fluctuation in the brain immediately before and after presentation of a stimulus, measured by electroencephalograph at the midline central scalp site (Cz). Results were presented as shown in Figures 3.25–3.27.

Exhibit 3.12

Independent Variable
1. Correct or incorrect pronunciation of English words

Dependent Variable
1. Event-related potentials (Cz scalp site)

Figure 3.25

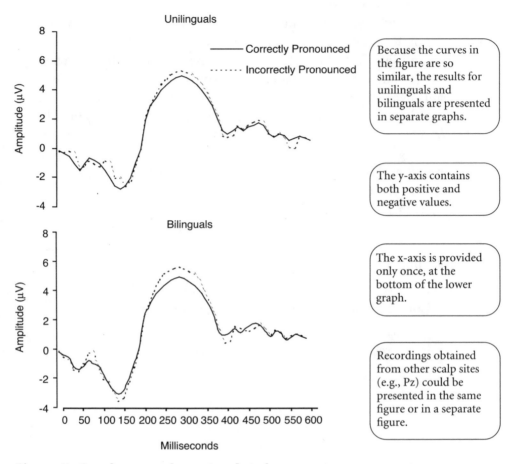

Figure X. Grand averaged event-related potentials for entire trial as a function of type of participant (unilingual or bilingual) and test word (pronounced correctly or incorrectly). Electroencephalographs were recorded from the Cz scalp site.

Because the curves in the figure are so similar, the results for unilinguals and bilinguals are presented in separate graphs.

The y-axis contains both positive and negative values.

The x-axis is provided only once, at the bottom of the lower graph.

Recordings obtained from other scalp sites (e.g., Pz) could be presented in the same figure or in a separate figure.

Figure 3.26

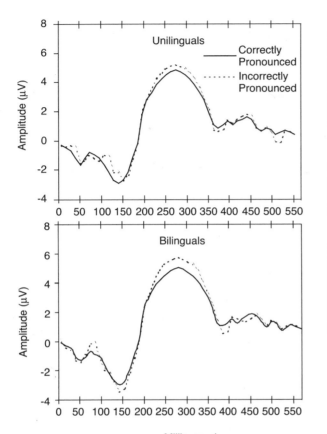

Optional top and right borders have been included. Tick marks on the top border help the reader to estimate values near the top part of the line graph.

Tick marks may be drawn on the right vertical axis (opposite the y-axis) as well.

The x-axis values are provided for each panel to make the graphs easier to read. The x-axis label and the legend need only be presented once, however.

Figure X. Grand averaged event-related potentials for entire trial as a function of type of participant (unilingual or bilingual) and test word (pronounced correctly or incorrectly). Electroencephalographs were recorded from the Cz scalp site.

Figure 3.27

This version of the figures shows that if the lines are close together, the interpretability of the graph suffers.

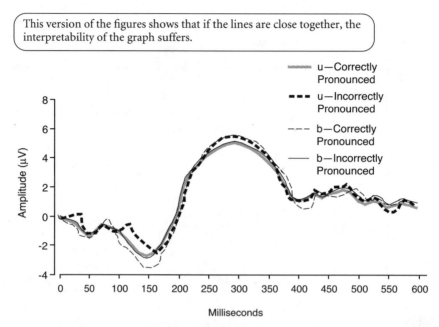

Figure X. Grand averaged event-related potentials for entire trial as a function of type of participant (unilingual or bilingual) and test word (pronounced correctly or incorrectly). Electroencephalographs were recorded from the Cz scalp site. u = unilinguals; b = bilinguals.

When there are a lot of lines to present in a single graph, it may be better to start the data points a bit farther from the y-axis, as was done here. This may make it easier to read values for the first data point.

Example 3.13

Two researchers wished to examine electrophysiological responses when identifying scrambled words after having named or spelled the word. In the first phase of the study, 20 participants were asked to look at a screen on which words were presented for a brief period. Immediately before the word was presented, a computer voice asked the participant to say the word out loud or to spell it out.

In the second phase of the study, electrophysiological recordings were taken with tin electrodes. The same words were presented as in the first phase, except this time the words were scrambled. ERPs were measured at three scalp sites—Fz (frontal), Cz (central), and Pz (parietal)—and presented as shown in Figure 3.28.

Exhibit 3.13

Independent Variable
1. Word identification (naming the word, spelling the word)

Dependent Variables
1. ERPs taken at location Fz
2. ERPs taken at location Cz
3. ERPs taken at location Pz

Figure 3.28

Often the y-axis is not included on each graph when numerous event-related-potential graphs are being presented.

Named   Spelled

Fz

Cz

Pz

It is common practice to reverse the y-axis scale when presenting event-related potentials such that negative values are above the x-axis and positive values are below the x-axis. This should be noted in the figure caption.

15 μV

0   800   ms

This is the negative symbol.

Figure X. Grand average event-related potentials (as measured in Phase 2 of the study) for scrambled words that were named or spelled out in Phase 1 of the study. Negativity is up on this figure (the solid line represents 0).

The zero reference line (x-axis) of the graphs has been noted in the figure caption.

Checklist of Effective Elements for All Figures

- All text in figure uses the same style font (sans serif).
- Font sizes within a figure do not vary by more than 4 points.
- Text in the caption uses the same font as the text of the manuscript.
- The caption is typed double-spaced.
- Figure captions are descriptive (i.e., they describe the variables of interest and other important information, such as what abbreviations mean).
- Figure captions are listed on a separate page.
- Lines are thick enough to be clear after reduction.
- Similar figures within the same manuscript have a similar appearance.
- Figures are referred to in the text using the figure number.

Checklist of Effective Elements for Line Graphs

- In axis labels and titles, the first letter of the first word and all major words are capitalized.
- In legends, the first letter of the first word and all major words are capitalized.
- The dependent variable is on the vertical (y) axis.
- The independent variable is on the horizontal (x) axis.
- The y-axis/x-axis length ratio is appropriate (usually the y-axis should be two thirds to three quarters the length of the x-axis).
- Axes are clearly labeled.
- Axis labels are parallel to the axes, if possible.
- Positive values on the x-axis increase to the right, whereas those on the y-axis increase up.
- Negative values on the x-axis increase to the left, whereas those on the y-axis increase down.
- There are no more than four lines or curves per graph.
- The legend is presented within figure boundaries.
- Lines representing the different independent variables within the graph can be clearly differentiated from one another.
- Symbols marking data points are the same size as the smallest lowercase letters in the graph.

CHAPTER 4

Plots

Plots are figures that present individual data points as a function of axis variables. We describe three types of plots: the scatter plot, the group centroids plot, and multidimensional scaling.

Scatter Plot

What Type of Data Is Presented?

Scatter plots present values of single events as a function of two variables scaled along the x- and y-axes. The purpose of the plot is usually to explore the relationship between two variables; for instance, a linear relationship may be indicated if the data points are clustered along the diagonal.

Example 4.1

A researcher wished to investigate the relationship between age and vocabulary size. The participants were 70 individuals, 10 from each decade between ages 10 and 80. Participants completed a standardized vocabulary test. Figures 4.1–4.3 present the results.

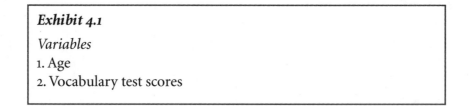

Exhibit 4.1

Variables
1. Age
2. Vocabulary test scores

Figure 4.1

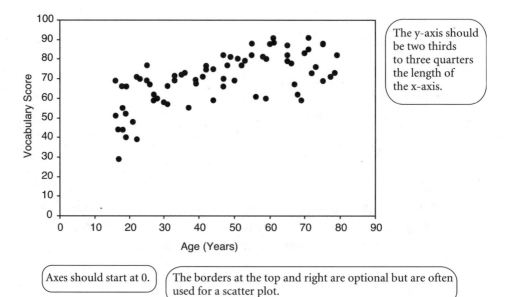

The y-axis should be two thirds to three quarters the length of the x-axis.

Axes should start at 0.

The borders at the top and right are optional but are often used for a scatter plot.

Figure X. Vocabulary scores as a function of participant age.

Plot symbols should be approximately the same size as a lowercase letter in the text used on the figure.

Figure 4.2

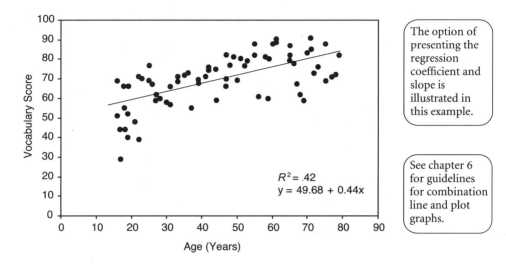

The option of presenting the regression coefficient and slope is illustrated in this example.

See chapter 6 for guidelines for combination line and plot graphs.

Figure X. Vocabulary scores as a function of participant age.

Figure 4.3

This scatter plot has no top or right borders.

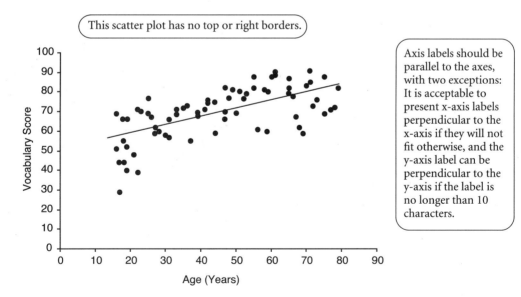

Axis labels should be parallel to the axes, with two exceptions: It is acceptable to present x-axis labels perpendicular to the x-axis if they will not fit otherwise, and the y-axis label can be perpendicular to the y-axis if the label is no longer than 10 characters.

Figure X. Vocabulary scores as a function of participant age.

Example 4.2

The Example 4.1 researcher expanded the previous study to include an investigation of the relationship between age and reading comprehension as well as between age and vocabulary size. The participants were the same 70 individuals, 10 from each decade between ages 10 and 80. Participants completed a standardized reading comprehension test in addition to the standardized vocabulary test. Figure 4.4 presents the findings.

Exhibit 4.2

Variables
1. Age
2. Vocabulary test scores
3. Reading comprehension test scores

Figure 4.4

This figure presents data for two linear relationships (using the same values on the y-axis) and their regression lines.

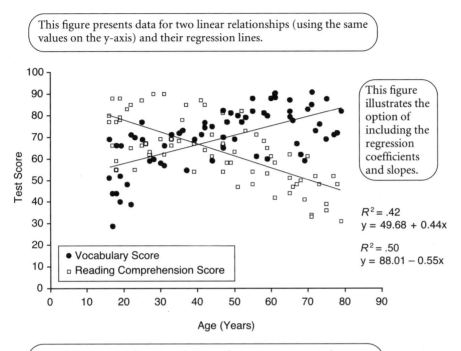

This figure illustrates the option of including the regression coefficients and slopes.

$R^2 = .42$
$y = 49.68 + 0.44x$

$R^2 = .50$
$y = 88.01 - 0.55x$

To enhance comprehension when two data sets are presented on a scatter plot, one set should use a closed shape (e.g., ●), and the other set should use an open shape (e.g., □).

Figure X. Vocabulary test scores and reading comprehension test scores as a function of participant age.

The legend should be placed within the boundaries of the axes.

Although differences between various symbols or lines may be observable on the computer monitor, these differences may not show up once the graph has been printed. Legibility can be verified by checking a laser printout.

Group Centroids Plot

What Type of Data Is Presented?

Group centroids plots are used to present the results of discriminant function analyses. This type of plot illustrates the extent to which the obtained functions discriminate among groups. Each group in the analysis is represented by a point in the plot. The further away the points are from each other in the plot, the more discriminability has been achieved in the analysis.

Example 4.3

A researcher was interested in the factors that predict the extent to which full-time high school students engage in part-time employment. The researcher surveyed 225 high school students and measured several predictor variables: family income, career goals, level of extracurricular participation, need for achievement, and need for affiliation. The researcher conducted a discriminant function analysis and presented a group centroids plot (Figure 4.5) as part of the written summary of the results.

Exhibit 4.3

Independent Variables
1. Family income
2. Career goals
3. Level of extracurricular participation
4. Need for achievement
5. Need for affiliation

Dependent Variable
1. Number of hours of part-time employment per week

Figure 4.5

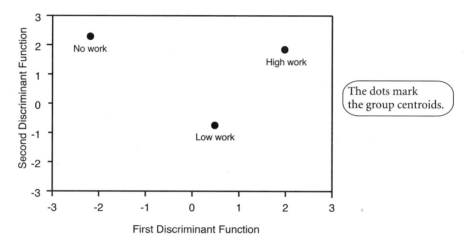

Figure X. Plots of three group centroids on two discriminant functions derived from family income, career goals, level of extracurricular participation, need for achievement, and need for affiliation.

Multidimensional Scaling

What Type of Data Is Presented?

Multidimensional scaling refers to a class of techniques (e.g., individual differences multidimensional scaling, or INDSCAL) that involve presenting similar points or stimuli close together in a multidimensional space and those that are dissimilar far apart.

Example 4.4

A researcher wished to study the perceived cause of maternal feelings in a sample of women with at least one child. The researcher first conducted a pilot study to identify a list of causes for maternal feelings. Once she had a list of causes, she asked a second group of participants to rate how each cause was similar to every other cause.

These pairs of causes were presented in random pairs to each participant. Multidimensional scaling was used to analyze the data (see Figures 4.6 and 4.7).

Exhibit 4.4

Variables

1. Amount of time able to spend with child
2. Amount of time spent at hospital
3. Age of mother
4. Whether child was breastfed
5. Complications during childbirth
6. Desire to have a child
7. Emotional support
8. Family upbringing
9. Financial support
10. Instinct
11. Knowledge
12. Necessity
13. Personality
14. Role of partner

Figure 4.6

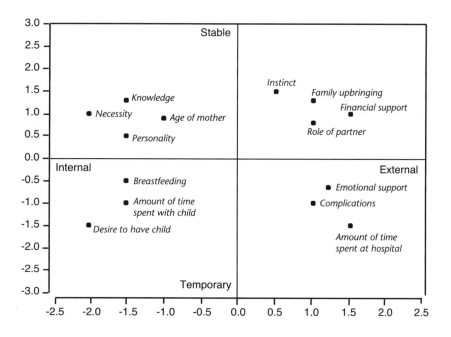

Figure X. Multidimensional analysis of perceived attributions for maternal behavior.

Figure 4.7

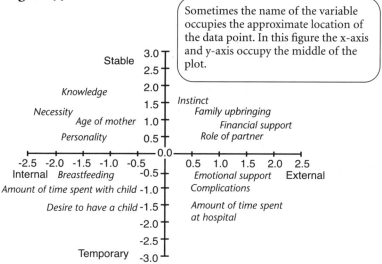

Sometimes the name of the variable occupies the approximate location of the data point. In this figure the x-axis and y-axis occupy the middle of the plot.

Figure X. Two-dimensional preference map based on multidimensional scaling of analysis of perceived attributions for 14 maternal behaviors.

Checklist of Effective Elements for All Figures

- All text in figure uses the same style font (sans serif).
- Font sizes within a figure do not vary by more than 4 points.
- Text in the caption uses the same font as the text of the manuscript.
- The caption is typed double-spaced.
- Figure captions are descriptive (i.e., they describe the variables of interest and other important information, such as what abbreviations mean).
- Figure captions are listed on a separate page.
- Lines are thick enough to be clear after reduction.
- Similar figures within the same manuscript have a similar appearance.
- Figures are referred to in the text using the figure number.

Checklist of Effective Elements for Plots

- In axis labels and titles, the first letter of the first word and all major words are capitalized.
- In legends, the first letter of the first word and all major words are capitalized.
- Text inside the plot has only the first letter of the first word capitalized.
- The y-axis/x-axis length ratio is appropriate (usually the y-axis should be two-thirds to three-quarters the length of the x-axis).
- Axes are clearly labeled.
- Axis labels are parallel to the axes, if possible.
- Zero points are indicated on the axes.
- Data points are represented by symbols that are approximately the same size as lowercase letters used in text on the figure.
- The legend is presented within figure boundaries.
- Regression coefficients and slopes are included for scatter plots if desired.

CHAPTER 5

Drawings

Drawings are illustrations of different aspects of research. This chapter discusses the presentation of apparatus illustrations, maps, questionnaire items, stimuli illustrations, hand drawings, and handwriting.

Apparatus

What Type of Information Is Presented?

Drawings can be used to illustrate characteristics of the apparatus used in experiments. Sometimes these drawings represent the apparatus alone (Example 5.1), and sometimes they represent the position of a participant in relation to the apparatus (Example 5.2).

Example 5.1

A researcher was interested in the effect of rewards on studying behavior. The researcher devised an apparatus that delivered either a chocolate candy or a nickel (5 cents, which was the monetary value of the chocolate candy) each time a participant correctly answered a study question. The researcher recruited 40 college students as participants. All of the students studied a given text and answered questions during the 2-hr experimental session. Half of the participants received a chocolate candy for every correct answer, and the other half received a nickel. The researcher included a drawing of the apparatus in his report (Figures 5.1 and 5.2).

Exhibit 5.1

Independent Variable
1. Type of reward (candy, nickel)

Dependent Variable
1. Number of correct responses to study questions

Figure 5.1

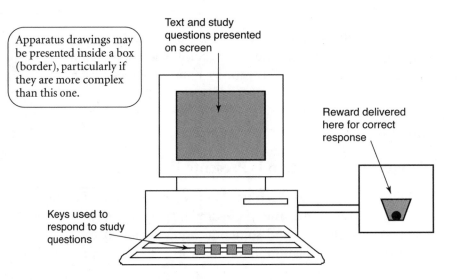

Figure X. Apparatus devised to deliver rewards for correct answers to study questions.

Figure 5.2

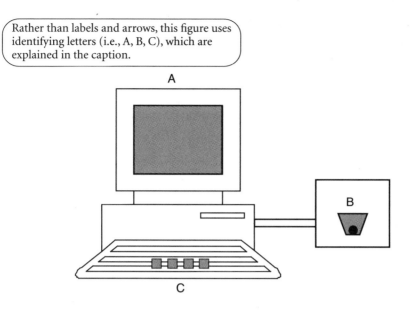

Rather than labels and arrows, this figure uses identifying letters (i.e., A, B, C), which are explained in the caption.

A

B

C

Figure X. Apparatus devised to deliver rewards for correct answers to study questions. A: Text and study questions presented on screen. B: Reward delivered here for correct response. C: Keys used to respond to study questions.

Example 5.2

A researcher studied infants' understanding of gravity in a sample of 24 six-month-old infants. The procedure involved dropping a ball behind a screen as the infants watched. The ball either reappeared at the bottom of the screen (as would be expected given an understanding of gravity) or did not reappear (the surprise condition). The researcher measured the infants' gaze duration, or how long they looked at the location where the ball should have reappeared. Figure 5.3 is a drawing of the apparatus and participants' locations.

Figure 5.3

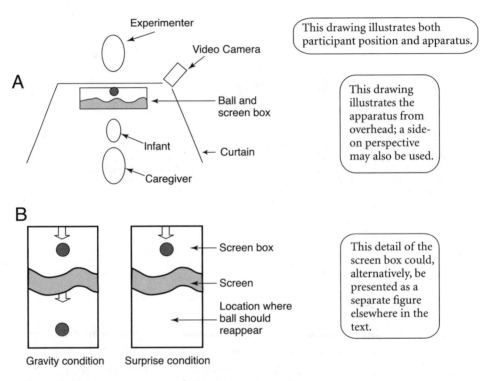

This drawing illustrates both participant position and apparatus.

This drawing illustrates the apparatus from overhead; a side-on perspective may also be used.

This detail of the screen box could, alternatively, be presented as a separate figure elsewhere in the text.

Figure X. Apparatus used to measure gaze duration. A: Arrangement of infant and experimenter in testing room. B: Detail of ball and screen box for gravity condition (ball reappears when dropped behind screen) and surprise condition (ball does not reappear when dropped behind screen).

Maps

What Type of Information Is Presented?

Maps are used to present spatial data. In psychology, maps are sometimes used to illustrate data as a function of geographic location (but only if geographic location is an important aspect of the study).

Example 5.3

A team of researchers investigated cognitive development in Santay Province, Martat (a fictional country), an area known to have high levels of pesticide runoff in the groundwater. The researchers devised a culturally appropriate test of cognitive development, standardized with 6-year-old children in a nonagricultural neighboring province, and administered it to 6-year-old children in each county of Santay Province. As part of their research summary, the researchers presented a map of Santay Province depicting average number of months of cognitive delay by county (Figures 5.4 and 5.5).

Exhibit 5.3

Variable
1. Cognitive development test scores

Figure 5.4

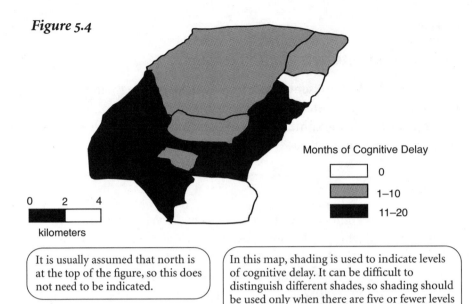

Months of Cognitive Delay

- ☐ 0
- ▨ 1–10
- ■ 11–20

0   2   4
kilometers

It is usually assumed that north is at the top of the figure, so this does not need to be indicated.

In this map, shading is used to indicate levels of cognitive delay. It can be difficult to distinguish different shades, so shading should be used only when there are five or fewer levels of the variable mapped.

Figure X. Map showing average number of months of cognitive delay for samples of 6-year-olds tested in each county in Santay Province, Martat.

Figure 5.5

In this map, patterns are used to indicate levels of cognitive delay. Blacker designs indicate higher levels of the variable mapped (i.e., cognitive delay).

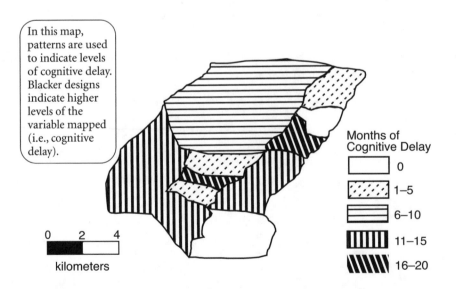

Months of Cognitive Delay

- ☐ 0
- ▨ 1–5
- ▤ 6–10
- ▥ 11–15
- ▨ 16–20

0   2   4
kilometers

Figure X. Map showing average number of months of cognitive delay for samples of 6-year-olds tested in each county in Santay Province, Martat.

Example 5.4

The Example 5.3 researchers were also interested in the native languages spoken in Santay Province. They collected information about which languages were spoken in the different regions and presented their findings in a map (Figure 5.6).

Exhibit 5.4

Variables
1. Tali language
2. Lingit language
3. Hon-opa language
4. Stax language

Figure 5.6

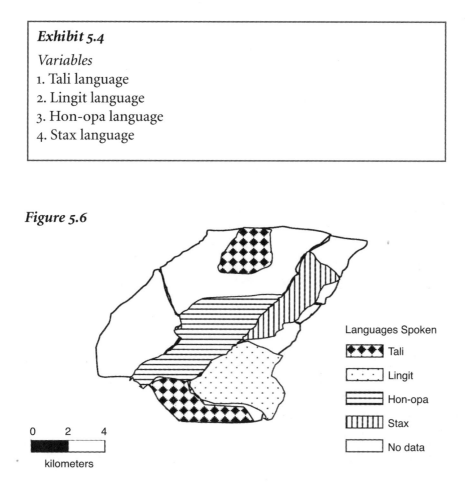

Figure X. Map showing languages spoken in Santay Province, Martat.

Questionnaires

What Type of Information Is Presented?

If a study involves the use of a new or unusual questionnaire, the researcher may choose to present part or all of the questionnaire as a figure. Doing so provides readers with information about the precise format and presentation of the questionnaire.

Example 5.5

Two developmental researchers investigated children's perceptions of sarcastic speech. The researchers were interested in the extent to which children perceived that sarcastic speakers were intending to be mean. The participants were 22 children age 6 years, 22 children age 7 years, and 24 children age 8 years. The children watched six short video segments depicting common events. Half of the video segments ended with a speaker making a sarcastic remark, and half ended with a speaker making a literal remark. The children were then asked to use a 5-point "face scale" to rate how mean they thought the speaker intended to be. In the written summary of this study, the researchers presented the face scale as a figure (see Figure 5.7).

Exhibit 5.5

Independent Variables
1. Age group (6, 7, 8 years old)
2. Type of remark (sarcastic, literal)

Dependent Variable
1. Face scale ratings

Figure 5.7

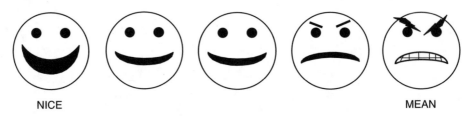

NICE   MEAN

Figure X. Face scale presented to children after each video segment.

Stimuli

What Type of Information Is Presented?

Drawings can be used to illustrate the types of stimuli used in experiments. These drawings usually illustrate what the stimuli looked like (Example 5.6). Sometimes, however, it is necessary to represent the way the stimuli were presented across time (Example 5.7) or to depict the motion of stimuli (Example 5.8).

Example 5.6

A researcher studying depression was particularly interested in information processing in depressed individuals. In this experiment, the researcher compared performance in picture naming of a group of 25 individuals in treatment for depression with a control group of 25 individuals who had never been depressed. The picture stimuli were line drawings of 40 objects with positive attributes and 40 with negative attributes. The researcher hypothesized that the depressed participants would take longer to name the negative objects than the control participants and that naming times would be equivalent for the two groups for the positive objects. The line drawings of objects were presented on a computer screen one at a time, and participants were asked to name them aloud as quickly and as accurately as they could. Figure 5.8 provides examples of the stimuli.

Exhibit 5.6

Independent Variables
1. Positivity of objects (positive, negative)
2. Depression (depressed, nondepressed)

Dependent Variable
1. Picture naming latency in milliseconds

Figure 5.8

A

B

Figure X. Sample line drawings presented in naming task. A: Negative objects (needle, handcuffs). B: Positive objects (money, bread).

Example 5.7

A researcher interested in working memory wanted to determine whether working memory was specific to different types of information. For instance, do people have working memory for mathematical information that is somewhat separate from working memory for nonmathematical (e.g., general knowledge) information? To investigate this issue, the researcher devised a dual-task procedure that required participants to draw heavily on their working memory resources (with a primary task) and enabled the researcher to see the effects this had on a separate (secondary) task.

The primary task involved remembering numbers, and the secondary task involved answering questions. The primary task had two levels: Participants remembered either one number (low load) or five numbers (high load). The secondary task also had two conditions: Participants answered either a mathematics question or a general knowledge question. The researcher hypothesized that performance on the mathematics questions would be poorer in the high-load condition than in the low-load condition and that performance on the general knowledge question would be less negatively affected by high load. The researcher's report included a drawing of the trial sequence (see Figures 5.9–5.13).

Exhibit 5.7

Independent Variables
1. Memory load (low, high)
2. Type of question (mathematics, general knowledge)

Dependent Variable
1. Number of questions answered correctly

Figure 5.9

Trial sequences can be illustrated in a number of ways; Figures 5.9–5.13 are some examples.

Figure X. Sequence of events in sample trials in the experiment.
A: Sequence of events in low-memory load condition. B: Sequence of
events in high-memory load condition.

Figure 5.10

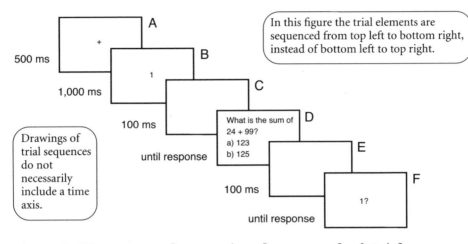

In this figure the trial elements are sequenced from top left to bottom right, instead of bottom left to top right.

Drawings of trial sequences do not necessarily include a time axis.

Figure X. Time course of events in a low-memory load trial. In a high-memory load trial, five digits would be presented at B, instead of one. This example trial also involves a mathematics question (at D). For a general knowledge trial, that question would refer to a nonmathematical concept. A: Fixation point. B: Memory task item. C: Blank screen. D: Mathematics or general knowledge question. E: Blank screen. F: Memory task probe.

Figure 5.11

This example illustrates the option of combining a table and drawings to present trial sequence information.

	Trial sequence			
Duration and event	Low load, mathematics	Low load, general	High load, mathematics	High load, general
500 ms: Fixation point	+	+	+	+
1,000 ms: Memory task item	1	1	1 5 6 9 8	1 5 6 9 8
100 ms: Blank screen				
Until response: Math or general question	What is the sum of 24 + 99? a) 123 b) 125	What is the capital of Canada? a) Toronto b) Ottawa	What is the sum of 24 + 99? a) 123 b) 125	What is the capital of Canada? a) Toronto b) Ottawa
100 ms: Blank screen				
Until response: Memory task probe	1 ?	1 ?	1 ?	1 ?

Figure X. Trial sequence used as a function of memory load and question.

Figure 5.12

This figure presents the trial sequence horizontally, from left to right.

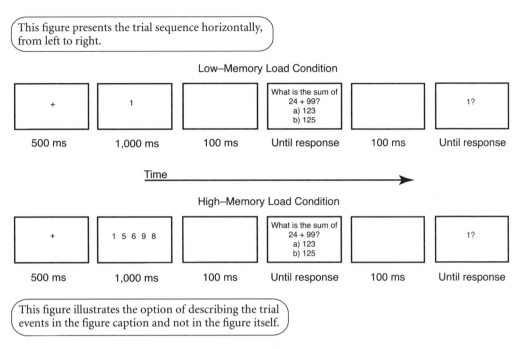

Low–Memory Load Condition

+	1		What is the sum of 24 + 99? a) 123 b) 125		1?
500 ms	1,000 ms	100 ms	Until response	100 ms	Until response

Time ──────────────────────→

High–Memory Load Condition

+	1 5 6 9 8		What is the sum of 24 + 99? a) 123 b) 125		1?
500 ms	1,000 ms	100 ms	Until response	100 ms	Until response

This figure illustrates the option of describing the trial events in the figure caption and not in the figure itself.

Figure X. Sequence of events during the low–memory load and high–memory load trials. Participants fixated on the cross (first panels) and then were presented with the memory task items. After a blank screen, the math (presented in the figure) or general knowledge question was presented until participants responded. After a second blank screen, the memory task probe item was presented, and participants indicated whether they had seen that item at the beginning of that particular trial.

Figure 5.13

This figure depicts the trial sequence on a time line or axis. This option should be used only when the trial events are quite conventional and have no unusual elements that might require illustration.

500 ms Fixation	1,000 ms Memory task item	100 ms Blank	Question response	100 ms Blank	Memory task response	TIME AXIS

Figure X. The timeline for each trial in the present experiment.

Example 5.8

A researcher investigated how video game playing experience influenced people's ability to track moving objects. The participants, 70 male college students, were asked to report their video game playing habits and were then divided into high-experience and low-experience groups, with 35 students in each. In the experiment, they were presented with target objects (either triangles or squares) on a computer screen. The objects then began to rotate, and the participants were asked to press a button when they thought the target had rotated back to its original orientation. The researcher hypothesized that the high-experience participants would make these judgments faster and more accurately than the low-experience participants. In her report the researcher included sample illustrations of the stimuli (see Figures 5.14 and 5.15).

Exhibit 5.8

Independent Variables
1. Video game playing experience (high, low)
2. Type of shape (triangle, square)

Dependent Variables
1. Orientation judgment reaction time
2. Orientation judgment accuracy

Figure 5.14

This figure illustrates how motion can be depicted in a drawing.

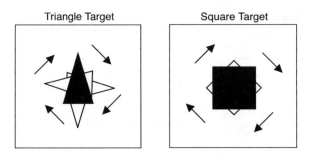

Triangle Target   Square Target

Figure X. The two shape conditions of the
present experiment. As illustrated,
rotation direction was clockwise.

Figure 5.15

This figure illustrates another way of depicting motion in a drawing. Here, rotation speed is depicted.

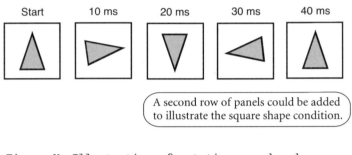

A second row of panels could be added to illustrate the square shape condition.

```
Figure X. Illustration of rotation speed and
direction of rotation for objects in the
experiment.
```

Hand Drawings and Handwriting

What Type of Information Is Presented?

Samples of hand drawings or handwriting can be presented as figures. These might be children's drawings (Example 5.9) or drawings by individuals from special populations. Similarly, handwriting samples might be presented to illustrate the writing of children (Example 5.10) or of individuals from special populations or to show portions of historical documents.

Example 5.9

Researchers interested in how children imagine "scary monsters" asked 20 young children (ages 4 and 5 years) and 20 older children (ages 7 and 8 years) to draw pictures of scary monsters. Each child was given white paper and 12 different colored markers and was asked to draw a picture. The researchers examined the pictures for similarity in terms of three criteria: (a) features, (b) spatial aspects (e.g., size, position on paper), and (c) colors. As part of their written description of the study, the researchers included two sample drawings (with permission; one by a younger child and one by an older child) to illustrate how similar many of the drawings were (Figure 5.16).

Exhibit 5.9

Independent Variable
1. Age group (4 and 5 years, 7 and 8 years)

Dependent Variables
1. Features of drawing
2. Spatial aspects of drawing
3. Colors in drawing

Figure 5.16

These drawings are presented in frames (boxes) to illustrate how the children composed the picture on the pages they were given. Often, however, hand drawings are presented without frames.

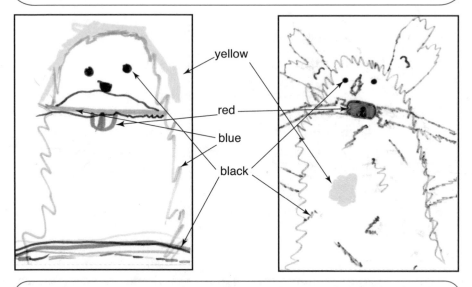

yellow
red
blue
black

Because pictures are usually published in black and white, it can be helpful to describe the colors used in drawings. This is particularly relevant in this study example because the researcher included colors used in the drawings as a dependent variable in the study.

Figure X. Drawings of "scary monsters" by a child age 4 years 7 months (left panel) and a child age 7 years 1 month (right panel).

Example 5.10

A graduate student investigating the development of children's writing skills was interested in mirror writing by young children. Mirror writing is backward, in the sense that words are written from right to left (instead of left to right), usually with each letter facing left instead of right. This type of writing is common among young children, and the researcher was interested in the extent to which early mirror writing (at ages 4 to 5 years) is associated with continued mirror writing and reading difficulties (at age 8 years).

The research conducted was a longitudinal study, in which 105 children between the ages of 4 and 5 were asked to produce 20 writing samples. These writing samples were coded for extent of mirror writing. When the children reached their eighth birthday, they were asked to provide 20 writing samples and were tested for level of reading skill (92 children from the original sample of 105 children participated at age 8 years). As part of the written summary of this research, the researcher produced (with permission) a figure showing early and later writing samples for one of the participants (Figure 5.17).

Exhibit 5.10

Variables
1. Extent of mirror writing at ages 4 to 5 years
2. Extent of mirror writing at age 8 years
3. Level of reading skill at age 8 years

Figure 5.17

For these handwriting samples, the writing is presented without a border (no box around). If the writing samples involved more words, then boxes around each sample might be an effective way to keep the samples separate.

When presenting two samples for comparison, as in this figure, the scale in each sample should be the same. That is, the samples should be presented so that relative size of the two samples is preserved.

NHoז

4 years, 5 months

John

8 years, 2 months

Figure X. Examples of writing samples produced by one participant. This participant showed mirror writing at age 4 years but not at age 8 years.

Checklist of Effective Elements for All Figures

- All text in figure uses the same style font (sans serif).
- Font sizes within a figure do not vary by more than 4 points.
- Text in the caption uses the same font as the text of the manuscript.
- The caption is typed double-spaced.
- Figure captions are descriptive (i.e., they describe the variables of interest and other important information, such as what abbreviations mean).
- Figure captions are listed on a separate page.

- Lines are thick enough to be clear after reduction.
- Similar figures within the same manuscript have a similar appearance.
- Figures are referred to in the text using the figure number.

Checklist of Effective Elements for Drawings

- Font size is large enough to withstand reduction before printing.
- All components of the drawing (especially any uncommon components) are clearly labeled, either on the drawing itself or in the figure caption.
- Shading is kept to a minimum and used only when contrast will aid comprehension.
- Similar drawings within the same manuscript have a similar appearance.

CHAPTER 6

Combination Graphs

What Type of Data Is Presented?

Combination graphs present two types of graphs within a single figure. For instance, a plot graph may include a regression line, a bar graph may present a line as well, and drawings or photographs may be incorporated within line or bar graphs.

Example 6.1

Researchers wished to study the influence of stress and violence on children's aggressive behavior. They asked 8-year-olds to answer questions regarding their stress level and the amount of violence they watched on television. Each child's parent was asked to rate the child's aggressive behavior. The researchers included a combination line graph and plot graph with their report (Figure 6.1).

Figure 6.1

> This figure combines a line graph and a plot graph. Regression lines indicate trends in the plotted data.

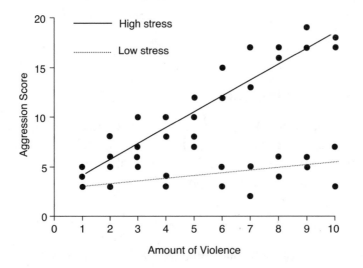

Figure X. Level of aggressive behavior as rated by parents of 8-year-old children as a function of stress level and amount of violence watched on TV. Computed slopes of regression line for level of violence and stress interaction are presented.

Example 6.2

A researcher wished to determine the ability of a sample of men to correctly match facial expressions. The 2 x 2 experimental design consisted of two kinds of targets, a male or a female face, and comparison faces that either matched the target facial expression or did not (the target sex was kept constant). Participants sat in front of a computer screen on which the target, followed by the comparison face, was presented. Participants indicated whether the faces matched by pressing a green button if they matched or a red button if they did not. The response times and the error rates of the participants were recorded and presented in a combination graph (see Figures 6.2–6.4).

Exhibit 6.2

Independent Variables
1. Target face (male, female)
2. Comparison face (similar, dissimilar facial expression)

Dependent Variables
1. Response time
2. Error rate

Figure 6.2

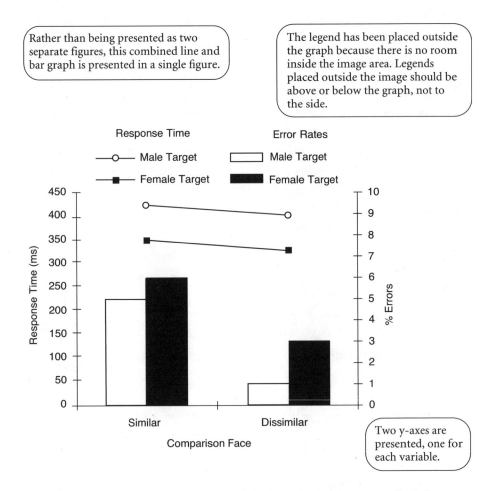

Rather than being presented as two separate figures, this combined line and bar graph is presented in a single figure.

The legend has been placed outside the graph because there is no room inside the image area. Legends placed outside the image should be above or below the graph, not to the side.

Two y-axes are presented, one for each variable.

Response Time

Error Rates

Male Target

Male Target

Female Target

Female Target

Response Time (ms)

% Errors

Similar

Dissimilar

Comparison Face

Figure X. Mean response times (lines) and error rates (bars) obtained in the similar and dissimilar comparison conditions of male and female facial expressions.

Figure 6.3

The % errors y-axis extends only a little higher than the maximum error rate obtained rather than spanning the full height of the graph.

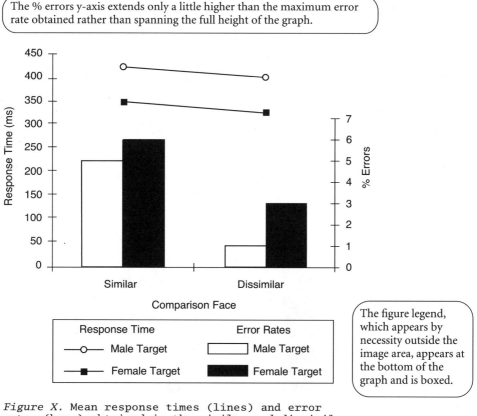

The figure legend, which appears by necessity outside the image area, appears at the bottom of the graph and is boxed.

Figure X. Mean response times (lines) and error rates (bars) obtained in the similar and dissimilar comparison conditions of male and female facial expressions.

The line graph symbols and bars are similar in appearance (i.e., open for male and closed for female).

Figure 6.4

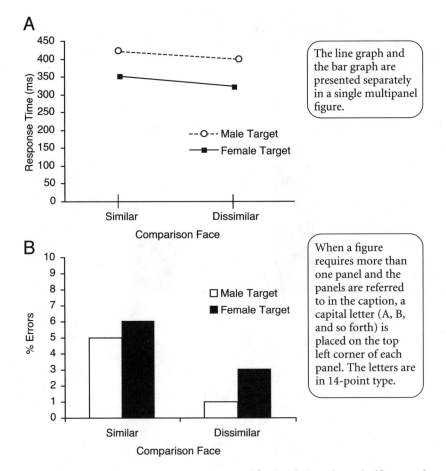

A

The line graph and the bar graph are presented separately in a single multipanel figure.

B

When a figure requires more than one panel and the panels are referred to in the caption, a capital letter (A, B, and so forth) is placed on the top left corner of each panel. The letters are in 14-point type.

Figure X. A: Mean response times obtained in the similar and dissimilar comparison conditions of male and female facial expressions. B: Mean error rates obtained in the similar and dissimilar comparison conditions of male and female facial expressions.

In the caption, each panel letter (A, B, etc.) is followed by a colon and a brief description of the panel. This is the preferred format.

Example 6.3

Two researchers wished to determine 4-year-old children's reaction time in correctly categorizing shapes. One of four shapes (diamond, parallelogram, square, or triangle) was presented on a screen for 1 s. The child indicated which shape he or she saw by pressing the corresponding shape on a response panel connected to a computer. The shapes were presented on the screen in random order and over several trials. The researchers recorded the response latency and the percentage of correct responses and later used this group as a comparison group in a study of the reaction times of children experiencing mild forms of visual disability. They presented the results in a bar graph that used drawings as x-axis labels, as shown in Figure 6.5.

Exhibit 6.3

Independent Variable
1. Identification of one of four shapes (square, parallelogram, diamond, triangle)

Dependent Variables
1. Response latency
2. Number of correct responses

Figure 6.5

This figure combines a bar graph and drawings.

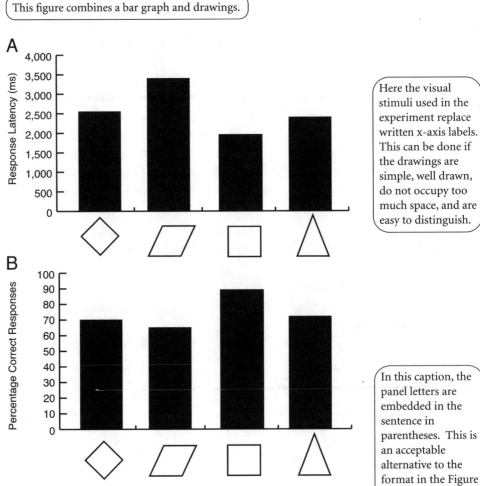

A

Here the visual stimuli used in the experiment replace written x-axis labels. This can be done if the drawings are simple, well drawn, do not occupy too much space, and are easy to distinguish.

B

In this caption, the panel letters are embedded in the sentence in parentheses. This is an acceptable alternative to the format in the Figure 6.4 caption.

Figure X. Reaction times (A) and accuracy (B) for identification of diamond, parallelogram, square, and triangle targets in a sample of children age 4 years.

Example 6.4

A researcher conducted a study of teenagers with various disorders and their reaction times in detecting which part of a face is missing. Each of five faces was presented for 0.5 s on the screen, and the participant indicated which part (if any) of the face was missing. One face was missing a right eye, one was missing a left eye, one was missing a left ear, one was missing a mouth, and one had nothing missing. The sample included 20 teenagers with attention deficit disorder (ADD), 20 with depression, 20 with obsessive-compulsive disorder (OCD), and 20 without any symptoms of a psychological disorder. The results are shown in Figure 6.6.

Exhibit 6.4

Independent Variable
1. Type of disorder (ADD, depression, OCD, no symptoms)
2. Identification of the missing part of five faces (nothing missing, no right eye, no left eye, no left ear, no mouth)

Dependent Variable
1. Reaction time to detect which part of a face is missing

Figure 6.6

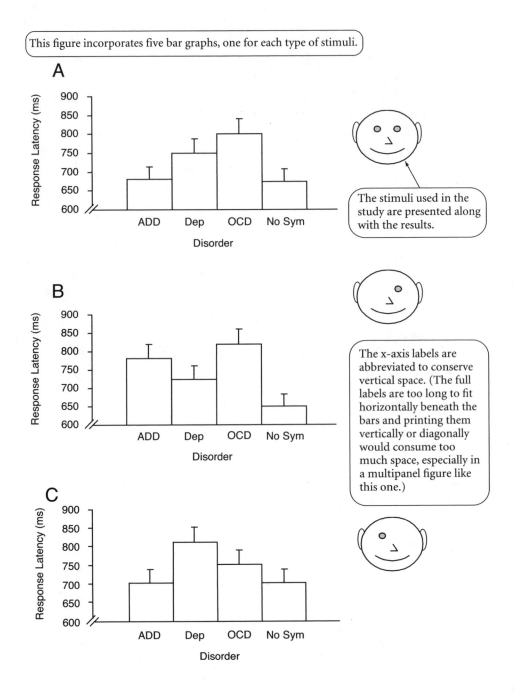

This figure incorporates five bar graphs, one for each type of stimuli.

A

Response Latency (ms) — y-axis: 600, 650, 700, 750, 800, 850, 900

x-axis (Disorder): ADD, Dep, OCD, No Sym

The stimuli used in the study are presented along with the results.

B

Response Latency (ms) — y-axis: 600, 650, 700, 750, 800, 850, 900

x-axis (Disorder): ADD, Dep, OCD, No Sym

The x-axis labels are abbreviated to conserve vertical space. (The full labels are too long to fit horizontally beneath the bars and printing them vertically or diagonally would consume too much space, especially in a multipanel figure like this one.)

C

Response Latency (ms) — y-axis: 600, 650, 700, 750, 800, 850, 900

x-axis (Disorder): ADD, Dep, OCD, No Sym

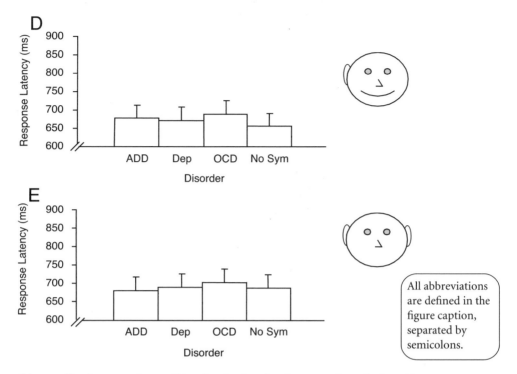

Figure X. Averaged results (and standard error bars) for the four groups of participants as a function of the five different stimuli: nothing missing on the face (A), no right eye (B), no left eye (C), no left ear (D), and no mouth (E). ADD = attention deficit disorder; Dep = depression; OCD = obsessive-compulsive disorder; No Sym = no symptoms.

Example 6.5

Three researchers wished to determine whether a sample of men could distinguish a baby's cry of pain from a cry of hunger. Male parents who had a 6-month-old baby at home were placed alone in a room and asked to fixate on a point. Five-second auditory sounds of a baby crying of pain or of hunger were randomly intermixed. Participants had to indicate on a keyboard immediately after hearing each sound which of the two types of sound they thought they heard. As part of their study, electroencephalographic signals were recorded from sites F_1, F_2, C_1, C_2, C_5, C_6, P_1, and P_2. Average measures of event-related potentials (ERP) were collected and presented as shown in Figure 6.7.

Independent Variable
1. Sound of baby crying (pain or hunger)

Dependent Variables
1. ERPs, F1 location
2. ERPs, F2 location
3. ERPs, C1 location
4. ERPs, C2 location
5. ERPs, C5 location
6. ERPs, C6 location
7. ERPs, P1 location
8. ERPs, P2 location

Figure 6.7

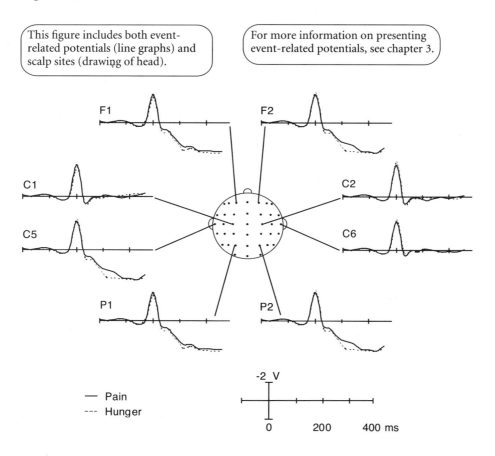

This figure includes both event-related potentials (line graphs) and scalp sites (drawing of head).

For more information on presenting event-related potentials, see chapter 3.

— Pain
--- Hunger

-2 V

0   200   400 ms

Figure X. Grand average event-related potentials for baby cries expressing pain or hunger in a sample of fathers.

Checklist of Effective Elements for All Figures

- All text in figure uses the same style font (sans serif).
- Font sizes within a figure do not vary by more than 4 points.
- Text in the caption uses the same font as the text of the manuscript.
- The caption is typed double-spaced.
- Figure captions are descriptive (i.e., they describe the variables of interest and other important information, such as what abbreviations mean).
- Figure captions are listed on a separate page.
- Lines are thick enough to be clear after reduction.
- Similar figures within the same manuscript have a similar appearance.
- Figures are referred to in the text using the figure number.

CHAPTER 7

Pie Graphs

What Type of Data Is Presented?

Pie graphs (sometimes referred to as *pie charts, cake charts, circle graphs, percentage graphs,* or *100% graphs*) are useful in illustrating percentages and proportions in relation to each other and to the whole. APA recommends that no more than five segments be shown in a single pie graph and that the largest segment (sometimes called a *slice, sector,* or *wedge*) start at 12 o'clock, with remaining sections following clockwise. Negative numbers cannot be illustrated in such a graph, and percentages over 100% should be avoided. In psychology, pie graphs are less common than other types of figures.

Example 7.1

A researcher wished to determine the extent to which the general population read psychology-related literature to seek help. The researcher asked 500 people to indicate the first source they would turn to when they had a psychology-related problem such as marriage trouble, problems with coworkers, lack of motivation, or problems with children. They were given one of the following choices to select from: academic psychology journals, textbooks, or books; popular psychology magazines; self-help books; advice columns in newspapers or magazines; and psychology Internet sites. The results were presented in a pie graph (Figures 7.1–7.3).

Exhibit 7.1

Variables
1. Consult academic psychology journals, textbooks, or books
2. Consult popular psychology magazines
3. Consult self-help books
4. Consult advice columns found in newspapers or magazines
5. Consult psychology Internet sites

Figure 7.1

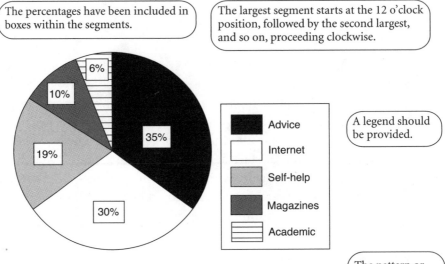

The percentages have been included in boxes within the segments.

The largest segment starts at the 12 o'clock position, followed by the second largest, and so on, proceeding clockwise.

A legend should be provided.

The pattern or shading in the smallest segments must enable them to be distinguishable from the other segments.

Figure X. For five types of psychology-related materials (advice columns; psychology Internet sites; self-help books; psychology magazines; or academic psychology journals, textbooks, or books), the percentage of individuals (N = 463) who indicated that the source would be their first choice for self-help.

Figure 7.2

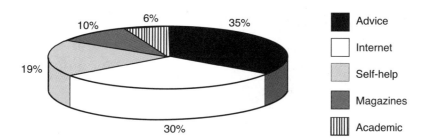

Figure X. For five types of psychology-related materials (advice columns; psychology Internet sites; self-help books; psychology magazines; or academic psychology journals, textbooks, or books), the percentage of individuals ($N = 463$) who indicated that the source would be their first choice for self-help.

Figure 7.3

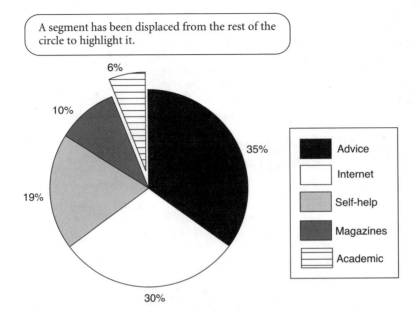

A segment has been displaced from the rest of the circle to highlight it.

Legend:
- Advice
- Internet
- Self-help
- Magazines
- Academic

Figure X. For five types of psychology-related materials (advice columns; psychology Internet sites; self-help books; psychology magazines; or academic psychology journals, textbooks, or books), the percentage of individuals ($N = 463$) who indicated that the source would be their first choice for self-help.

Checklist of Effective Elements for All Figures

- All text in figure uses the same style font (sans serif).
- Font sizes within a figure do not vary by more than 4 points.
- Text in the caption uses the same font as the text of the manuscript.
- The caption is typed double-spaced.
- Figure captions are descriptive (i.e., they describe the variables of interest and other important information, such as what abbreviations mean).
- Figure captions are listed on a separate page.
- Lines are thick enough to be clear after reduction.
- Similar figures within the same manuscript have a similar appearance.
- Figures are referred to in the text using the figure number.

Checklist of Effective Elements for Pie Graphs

- Segment labels are all horizontal.
- Pie segments can easily be distinguished from one another.
- There are no more than five segments in a single pie graph.
- A legend is provided that identifies the segments.
- Negative numbers are not illustrated.
- Percentages total 100%.

CHAPTER 8

Miscellaneous Graphs

Miscellaneous graphs are those that do not clearly fit the descriptions of the other graphs identified in this book. This chapter presents two types of graphs: the dendrogram and the stem-and-leaf plot.

Dendrograms

What Type of Data Is Presented?

A dendrogram presents the steps in a cluster analysis solution by illustrating which variables are combined to form clusters. Cluster analysis consists of a set of techniques used to identify the structure or grouping of a set of entities. Combined variables are connected using vertical lines. The dendrogram also presents the values of the distance coefficients for each step or vertical line.

Example 8.1

Two honors students wished to create a measure of "goofiness." They made up 10 items and decided to first test their measure on a sample of 150 students. They wished to determine the structure of their measure by conducting an agglomerative cluster analysis. As part of their results, they presented a dendrogram (see Figure 8.1).

Exhibit 8.1

Variables
Measure of goofiness:
1. Says silly things
2. Makes funny facial expressions
3. Cannot be serious for long
4. Frequently jokes
5. Has short attention span
6. Selects inappropriate conversation topics
7. Uses frequent hand gestures
8. Wants to be center of attention
9. Frequently laughs
10. Makes verbal noises (sound effects)

Figure 8.1

Figure X. Dendrogram for the Goofiness scale based on the results of an agglomerative cluster analysis.

Stem-and-Leaf Plots

What Type of Data Is Presented?

Stem-and-leaf plots present frequencies of raw data while maintaining all of the original data. Each line is referred to as a *stem* and consists of a number, a vertical line, and some more numbers, where appropriate. Each number on a stem to the left of the vertical line is referred to as the *stem label*, and each number to the right of the vertical line is called a *leaf*.

Example 8.2

A researcher interested in the relation between optimism and job performance conducted a meta-analysis to quantitatively determine the magnitude of this relation across numerous published studies. As part of her results, she presented the effect sizes found in the studies she incorporated in her meta-analysis in a stem-and-leaf plot, as shown in Figures 8.2 and 8.3.

> **Exhibit 8.2**
>
> *Variables*
> 1. Optimism
> 2. Job performance

Figure 8.2

```
1.7 |
1.6 | 1
1.5 |
1.4 |
1.3 | 3
1.2 |
1.1 | 9
1.0 | 2
0.9 | 14
0.8 |
0.7 | 9
0.6 | 0112
0.5 | 567
0.4 | 34
0.3 | 4589
0.2 | 033455789
0.1 | 45
0.0 | 02399
-0.0 | 023448
-0.1 | 23
-0.2 | 3467
-0.3 | 016
-0.4 | 8
-0.5 | 29
-0.6 | 34
-0.7 | 29
-0.8 | 2
-0.9 | 01
-1.0 | 4
-1.1 |
-1.2 | 2
-1.3 |
-1.4 |
-1.5 | 1
   . |
   . |
   . |
-2.3 | 8
```

The stem-and-leaf plot presents all of the raw data in simplified form. For instance, there were zero effect sizes with the values of 1.70 to 1.79; one effect size with the value of 1.33; and one with the value of 0.60, two with the value of 0.61, and one with the value of 0.62.

It is best to place the leaves in increasing or decreasing numerical order. (This figure presents the leaves in increasing numerical order.)

The caption should identify what the numbers in the stem labels and leaves represent.

To save space, three dots take the place of values from −1.6 to −2.2 here; there are no raw data for these stem labels.

Figure X. Stem-and-leaf plot of effect
sizes (*d*). Stem labels are the ones and
tenths places for each effect size.
Leaves are the hundredths place for each
effect size.

Figure 8.3

```
0    1.7 |
1    1.6 | 1
0    1.5 |
0    1.4 |
1    1.3 | 3
0    1.2 |
1    1.1 | 9
1    1.0 | 2
2    0.9 | 14
0    0.8 |
1    0.7 | 9
4    0.6 | 0112
3    0.5 | 567
2    0.4 | 34
4    0.3 | 4589
9    0.2 | 033455789
2    0.1 | 45
5    0.0 | 02399
6   -0.0 | 023448
2   -0.1 | 23
4   -0.2 | 3467
3   -0.3 | 016
1   -0.4 | 8
2   -0.5 | 29
2   -0.6 | 34
2   -0.7 | 29
1   -0.8 | 2
2   -0.9 | 01
1   -1.0 | 4
0   -1.1 |
1   -1.2 | 2
0   -1.3 |
0   -1.4 |
1   -1.5 | 1
0   -1.6 |
0   -1.7 |
0   -1.8 |
0   -1.9 |
0   -2.0 |
0   -2.1 |
0   -2.2 |
1   -2.3 | 8
```

This stem-and-leaf plot presents the frequencies to the left of each stem label; this is noted in the figure caption.

Figure X. Stem-and-leaf plot of effect sizes (*d*). Stem labels are the ones and tenths places for each effect size. Leaves are the hundredths place for each effect size. Frequencies of each effect size are presented to the left of the stem labels.

Checklist of Effective Elements for All Figures

- All text in figure uses the same style font (sans serif).
- Font sizes within a figure do not vary by more than 4 points.
- Text in the caption uses the same font as the text of the manuscript.
- The caption is typed double-spaced.
- Figure captions are descriptive (i.e., they describe the variables of interest and other important information, such as what abbreviations mean).
- Figure captions are listed on a separate page.
- Lines are thick enough to be clear after reduction.
- Similar figures within the same manuscript have a similar appearance.
- Figures are referred to in the text using the figure number.

CHAPTER 9

Charts

What Type of Data Is Presented?

Charts are used to present models (e.g., conceptual or theoretical models, structural equation models, confirmatory factor analysis models) and flowcharts. They are also used to present the results of mediator or moderator analyses, structural equation analyses, and confirmatory factor analyses. Charts consist of enclosed boxes, squares, or circles connected with straight or curved lines or arrows.

Example 9.1

A researcher conducted a case study of Company TA's communication lines between employees and their supervisors to identify the different ways individuals communicate with one another according to their level within the company. He created an organizational chart, as shown in Figure 9.1, to provide a visual presentation of the various levels within the organization.

Exhibit 9.1

Independent Variable
1. Occupation level within an organization

Dependent Variable
1. Communication style

Figure 9.1

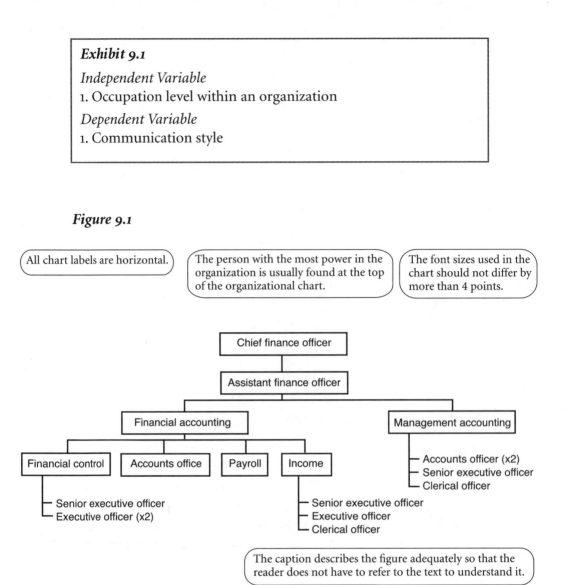

All chart labels are horizontal.

The person with the most power in the organization is usually found at the top of the organizational chart.

The font sizes used in the chart should not differ by more than 4 points.

Chief finance officer

Assistant finance officer

Financial accounting

Management accounting

Financial control

Accounts office

Payroll

Income

— Accounts officer (x2)
— Senior executive officer
— Clerical officer

— Senior executive officer
— Executive officer (x2)

— Senior executive officer
— Executive officer
— Clerical officer

The caption describes the figure adequately so that the reader does not have to refer to the text to understand it.

Figure X. Organizational structure of Company TA illustrating the direct lines of communication.

Example 9.2

A researcher designed a conceptual model of determinants of compliance with medication regimens in cancer patients. She supplemented her written description of the theoretical background and the various components of the model with a figure to help readers easily comprehend the model (see Figures 9.2–9.5).

Exhibit 9.2

Variables

1. Individual characteristics (personal variables, demographic variables)
2. Attitudes and beliefs regarding taking medication
3. Commitment to taking medication
4. Situational constraints (number of people living with, available time, support from others)
5. Intention to comply
6. Compliance (frequency of regular usage, number of times medication not taken)

Figure 9.2

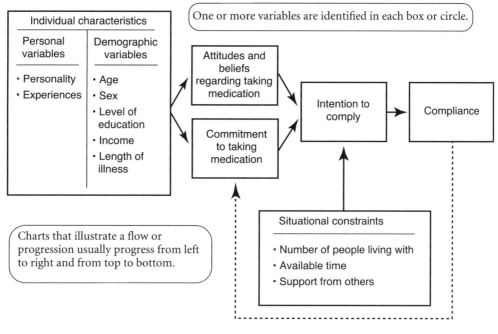

Figure X. Conceptual model of determinants of cancer patients' compliance in taking medication. Dashed arrow indicates the reciprocal nature of the model.

Figure 9.3

Conceptual or theoretical models can be drawn with a variety of shapes, but these should be meaningful. The meaning of the shapes can be explained in the figure caption.

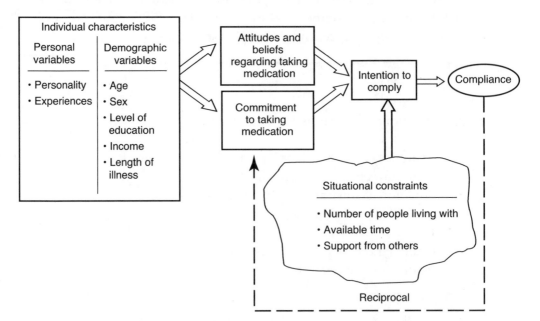

Figure X. Conceptual model of determinants of cancer patients' compliance in taking medication. Boxes represent preprescription measures (measures taken before medication was prescribed), ellipse represents postprescription measure, and squiggly box represents pre- and postprescription measures.

Figure 9.4

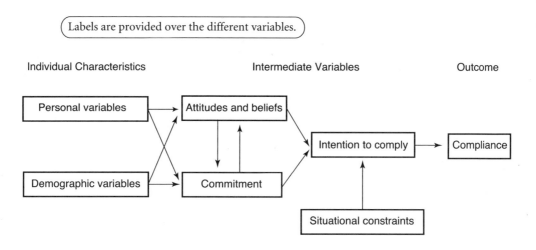

Labels are provided over the different variables.

Individual Characteristics   Intermediate Variables   Outcome

Figure X. Conceptual model of the three-component model of cancer patients' compliance in taking medication. *Personal variables* include personality and personal experiences; *demographic variables* include age, sex, level of education, income, and length of illness. *Attitudes and beliefs* and *commitment* are those related to taking medication. *Situational constraints* include number of people living with, available time, and support from others. *Intention to comply* is the extent to which an individual intends to take the medication regularly. *Compliance* reflects frequency of regular usage and number of times medication is not taken.

Figure 9.5

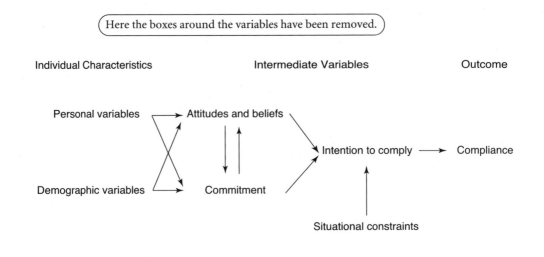

Here the boxes around the variables have been removed.

Individual Characteristics   Intermediate Variables   Outcome

Figure X. Conceptual model of the three-component model of cancer patients' compliance in taking medication. *Personal variables* include personality and personal experiences; *demographic variables* include age, sex, level of education, income, and length of illness. *Attitudes and beliefs* and *commitment* are those related to taking medication. *Situational constraints* include number of people living with, available time, and support from others. *Intention to comply* is the extent to which an individual intends to take the medication regularly. *Compliance* reflects frequency of regular usage and number of times medication not taken.

Example 9.3

A researcher wished to study three aspects of the theoretical model presented in Example 9.2. He wished to determine whether intention to comply is a mediator between attitudes regarding taking medication and frequency of regular usage of medication in cancer patients. He presented the results of the mediator analysis (using regression analyses) as shown in Figure 9.6.

Figure 9.6

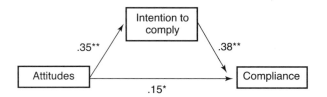

Figure X. Mediating role of intention to comply in explaining the relation between attitudes regarding taking medication and compliance.
*$p < .05$. **$p < .001$.

Example 9.4

A researcher was preparing a research proposal to study parts of the model presented in Example 9.2. She wished to study the effects of three variables—(a) personality (as measured by conscientiousness and learned resourcefulness), (b) commitment (consisting of affective and continuance commitment), and (c) acceptance of taking medication (as measured by beliefs and attitudes regarding taking medication)—on compliance (frequency of regular usage and number of times medication not taken). She included in her proposal a chart of the causal model she intended to test (Figure 9.7).

Exhibit 9.4

Latent Variable
1. Personality

Indicator Variables
1. Conscientiousness (x_1)
2. Learned resourcefulness (x_2)

Latent Variable
2. Commitment

Indicator Variables
3. Affective commitment (x_3)
4. Continuance commitment (x_4)

Latent Variable
3. Acceptance of taking medication

Indicator Variables
5. Attitudes regarding taking medication (x_5)
6. Beliefs regarding taking medication (x_6)

Latent Variable
4. Compliance

Indicator Variables
7. Frequency of regular usage (y_1)
8. Number of times medication not taken (y_2)

Figure 9.7

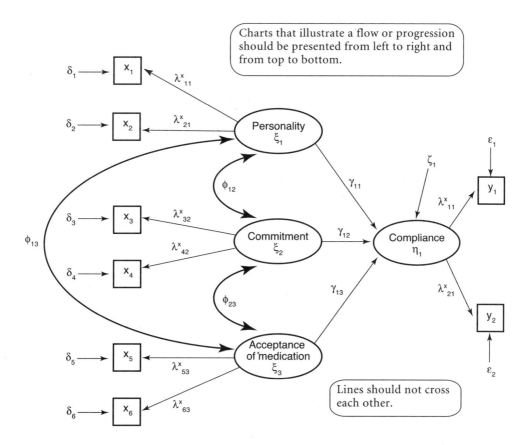

Charts that illustrate a flow or progression should be presented from left to right and from top to bottom.

Lines should not cross each other.

Figure X. Causal model of effects between personal attributes of an individual and compliance. x_1 = conscientiousness; x_2 = learned resourcefulness; x_3 = affective commitment; x_4 = continuance commitment; x_5 = attitudes regarding taking medication; x_6 = beliefs regarding taking medication; y_1 = frequency of regular usage; y_2 = number of times medication not taken.

Example 9.5

A researcher wished to study and test aspects of the theoretical model presented in Example 9.2. He wished to study the extent to which compliance (frequency of regular usage, number of times medication not taken) is influenced by intentions and whether this relation is moderated by situational constraints (number of people living with, available time, support from others). Furthermore, he believed that several variables may influence a person's intention to comply: personality, commitment to taking medication, and acceptance of taking medication. Personality variables of interest were conscientiousness and learned resourcefulness; commitment consisted of affective and continuance commitment; and acceptance of taking medication consisted of attitudes and beliefs regarding taking medication. The researcher first presented the conceptual model (see Figures 9.8 and 9.9). After conducting the study and structural equation analysis, he presented the standardized coefficients for the model as shown in Figures 9.10–9.13.

Exhibit 9.5

Latent Variable
1. Personality

Indicator Variables
1. Conscientiousness
2. Learned resourcefulness

Latent Variable
2. Commitment

Indicator Variables
3. Affective commitment
4. Continuance commitment

Latent Variable
3. Acceptance of taking medication

Indicator Variables
5. Beliefs regarding taking medication
6. Attitudes regarding taking medication

Indicator Variable
7. Measure of intention to comply

Latent Variable
4. Situational constraints

Indicator Variables
8. Number of people living with
9. Available time
10. Support from others

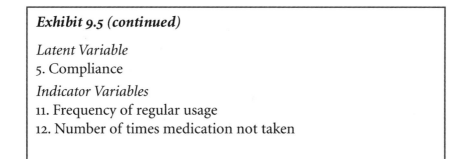

Exhibit 9.5 (continued)

Latent Variable

5. Compliance

Indicator Variables

11. Frequency of regular usage

12. Number of times medication not taken

Figure 9.8

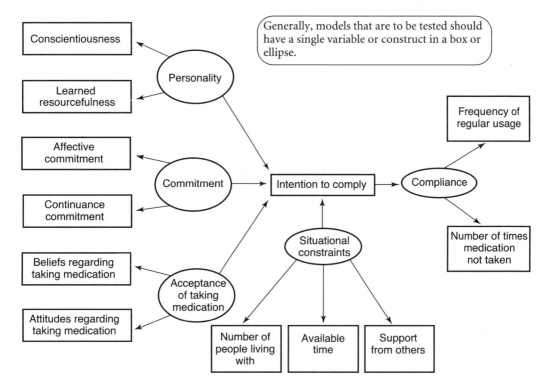

Figure X. Proposed model of cancer patients' compliance in taking medication.

Figure 9.9

Figure X. Model for cancer patients' compliance in taking medication.
P1 = conscientiousness; P2 = learned resourcefulness; C1 = affective
commitment; C2 = continuance commitment; A1 = beliefs regarding taking
medication; A2 = attitudes regarding taking medication; S1 = number of
people living with; S2 = available time; S3 = support from others;
CO1 = frequency of regular usage; CO2 = number of times medication not
taken. Latent constructs are shown in ellipses, and observed variables
are in rectangles.

Figure 9.10

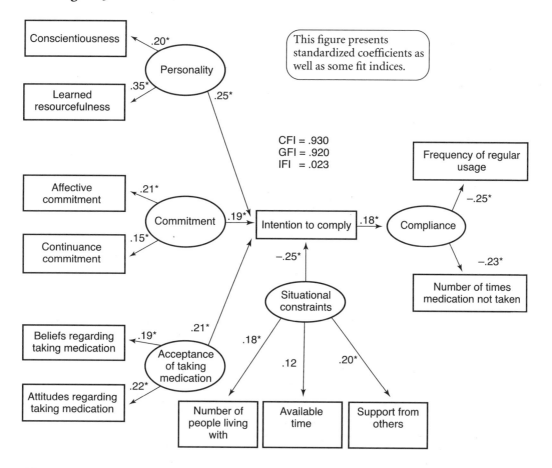

Figure X. Standardized coefficients for final model of cancer patients'
compliance in taking medication. CFI = comparative fit index; GFI =
goodness-of-fit index; IFI = incremental fit index. Latent constructs
are shown in ellipses, and observed variables are in rectangles.
*p < .05.

Figure 9.11

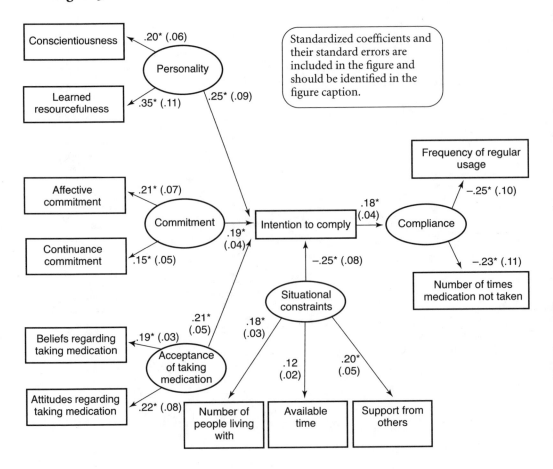

Figure X. Standardized coefficients for model of cancer patients'
compliance in taking medication. Standard errors are included in
parentheses. Comparative fit index = .93; goodness-of-fit index = .92;
incremental fit index = .023; root-mean-square residual = .91. Latent
constructs are enclosed in ellipses, and observed variables are
enclosed in boxes.
*p < .05.

Figure 9.12

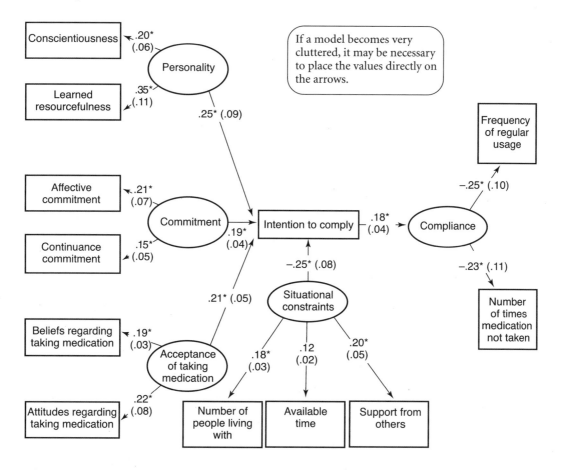

If a model becomes very cluttered, it may be necessary to place the values directly on the arrows.

Figure X. Standardized coefficients for model of cancer patients' compliance in taking medication. Standard errors are included in parentheses. Comparative fit index = .93; goodness-of-fit index = .92; incremental fit index = .023; root-mean-square residual = .91. Latent constructs are enclosed in ellipses, and observed variables are enclosed in boxes.
*p < .05.

Figure 9.13

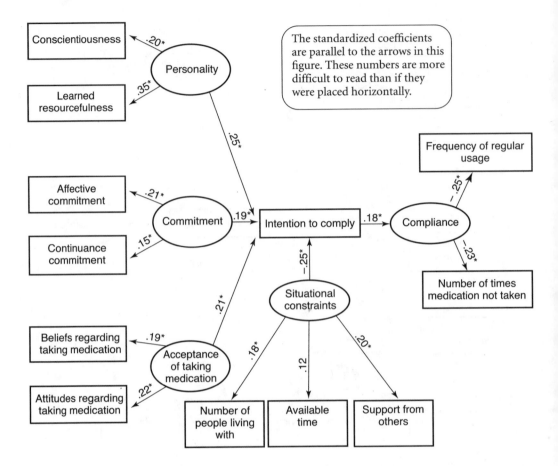

The standardized coefficients are parallel to the arrows in this figure. These numbers are more difficult to read than if they were placed horizontally.

Figure X. Standardized coefficients for model of cancer patients' compliance in taking medication.
*p < .05.

Example 9.6

Three researchers sought to explore some of the reasons parents place their children in private schools. They developed a decision tree that they believed parents follow when making such a decision. They drew a flowchart to depict the various decisions they believed parents make (Figures 9.14 and 9.15). A flowchart is a series of lines and text boxes to illustrate the steps involved in a procedure or decision.

Exhibit 9.6

Variables

1. Ideology in favor of private schooling
2. Perceived adequacy of public schooling
3. Close proximity of private school
4. Desire to use alternatives
5. Use of alternatives
6. Adequate financial resources
7. Decision to send children to public or private school

Figure 9.14

Figure X. Conceptual model of parents' decision-making process when choosing the type of schooling for their children.

Figure 9.15

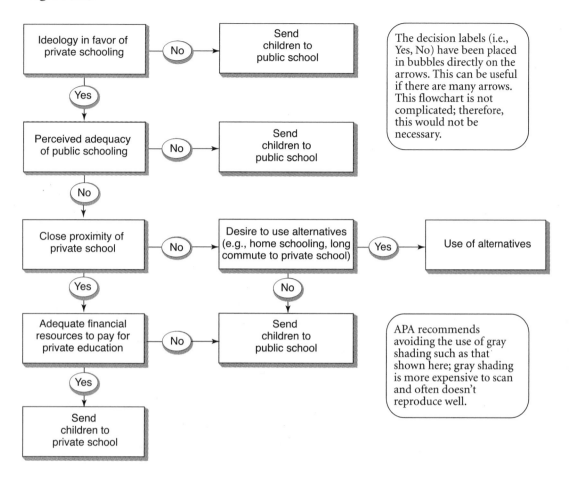

Ideology in favor of private schooling — No → Send children to public school

Yes ↓

Perceived adequacy of public schooling — No → Send children to public school

No ↓

Close proximity of private school — No → Desire to use alternatives (e.g., home schooling, long commute to private school) — Yes → Use of alternatives

Yes ↓

No ↓

Adequate financial resources to pay for private education — No → Send children to public school

Yes ↓

Send children to private school

The decision labels (i.e., Yes, No) have been placed in bubbles directly on the arrows. This can be useful if there are many arrows. This flowchart is not complicated; therefore, this would not be necessary.

APA recommends avoiding the use of gray shading such as that shown here; gray shading is more expensive to scan and often doesn't reproduce well.

Figure X. Conceptual model of parents' decision-making process when choosing the type of schooling for their children.

Example 9.7

A researcher wished to survey families living in an urban area to determine what percentages of parents living in affluent or poor neighborhoods perceived public schools to be adequate and how many sent their children to private schools. She presented the results of this survey in a figure, shown in Figure 9.16.

Exhibit 9.7

Independent Variable
1. Neighborhood (affluent, poor)

Dependent Variables
1. Perceived adequacy of public school (good, poor)
2. Child sent to private school (yes, no)

Figure 9.16

This kind of figure should be read from left to right.

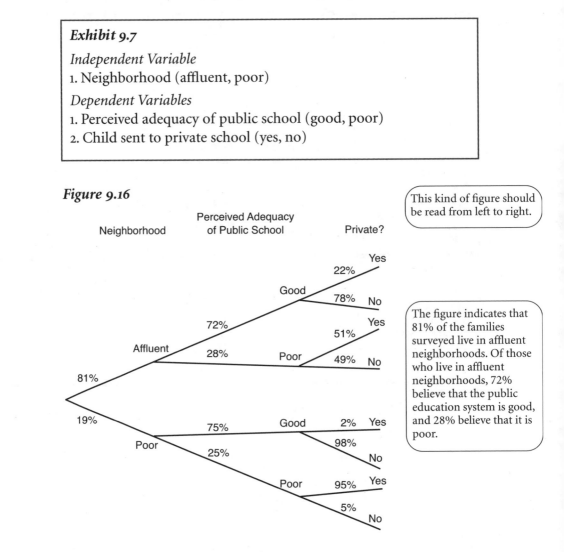

The figure indicates that 81% of the families surveyed live in affluent neighborhoods. Of those who live in affluent neighborhoods, 72% believe that the public education system is good, and 28% believe that it is poor.

Figure X. Percentage of parents (*N* = 841) who sent their children to private school as a function of their perceptions of the quality of public education and the type of neighborhood they lived in.

Checklist of Effective Elements for All Figures

- All text in figure uses the same style font (sans serif).
- Font sizes within a figure do not vary by more than 4 points.
- Text in the caption uses the same font as the text of the manuscript.
- The caption is typed double-spaced.
- Figure captions are descriptive (i.e., they describe the variables of interest and other important information, such as what abbreviations mean).
- Figure captions are listed on a separate page.
- Lines are thick enough to be clear after reduction.
- Similar figures within the same manuscript have a similar appearance.
- Figures are referred to in the text using the figure number.

Checklist of Effective Elements for Charts

- Charts read from left to right and top to bottom.
- Titles within charts have the first letter of the first word and all important words capitalized.
- Variables have only the first letter of the first word capitalized.
- Graphic elements are as simple and as consistent as possible within figures and across figures in the same manuscript.

CHAPTER 10

Photographs

What Type of Data Is Presented?

Photographs can be used to illustrate procedures or stimuli and to present brain images or slides of tissue slices. Photographs present certain problems. Most books and journals can publish photographs only in black and white, so the contrast must be very strong to be effectively reproduced in print. Some publishers, however, will print color photographs provided the author covers some or all associated costs. In their electronic form, photographs can require a considerable amount of storage (e.g., disk) space. Photographs should be used only for illustrations that would be very difficult to portray effectively with drawings (e.g., facial expressions, hand positions, and unusual three-dimensional objects).

Example 10.1

Two researchers wished to examine reaching behavior in younger and older adults. They were particularly interested in comparing reaching behavior for these two age groups for familiar and unfamiliar objects. The researchers recruited 30 younger adults (ages 25 to 35 years) and 30 older adults (ages 70 to 80 years). The target objects included six familiar objects and six unfamiliar objects. On each trial in the procedure, participants were asked to reach for and pick up one of the objects. The researchers devised an infrared camera system that measured three aspects of reaching behavior: arm speed, accuracy of arm angle, and grip aperture. The researchers examined how each of these aspects of reaching behavior was affected by age and by object familiarity. In their report the researchers presented photos of sample objects and reaches, as shown in Figure 10.1.

Exhibit 10.1

Independent Variables
1. Age group (younger, older adults)
2. Object familiarity (familiar, unfamiliar objects)

Dependent Variables
1. Arm speed
2. Accuracy of arm angle
3. Grip aperture

Figure 10.1

These photographs illustrate examples of the objects used in the experiment and the type of grasping behavior produced. These aspects of the study would be difficult to illustrate in drawings.

Familiar Object

Unfamiliar Object

Elements of side-by-side photographs should be proportional.

Figure X. Sample grips used for familiar and unfamiliar objects in the grasping task.

Example 10.2

A researcher studying how meaning information is activated in the brain was interested in whether specific semantic decisions and general semantic decisions activate the same brain areas. Past research implicated the left prefrontal cortex in semantic processing, and the researcher wanted to investigate whether specific semantic processing involves different areas than general semantic processing within the left prefrontal cortex. Participants were 32 right-handed adults. Half of the participants were asked to make specific semantic decisions (e.g., "Is it furniture?") for word targets. The other half of the participants were asked to make general semantic decisions (e.g., "Is it made by humans?") for word targets. In both conditions, participants indicated their responses by pressing a button with their right index finger (for "yes" responses) or their left index finger (for "no" responses). All participants made these decisions while undergoing functional magnetic resonance imaging (fMRI) so that the researcher could measure brain activity. The researcher used radiographs to illustrate his findings (Figure 10.2).

Exhibit 10.2

Independent Variable
1. Specificity of semantic decision (specific, general)

Dependent Variable
1. Brain activity in left prefrontal cortex

Figure 10.2

General Semantic Decision   Specific Semantic Decision

This figure illustrates the option of placing condition labels above the images.

Arrows are used to point to key areas.

Figure X. Transverse sections showing activation in the left prefrontal cortex in the two semantic decision conditions. Images are composites for 16 participants each and are displayed in radiographic convention (left hemisphere on right of image).

The radiographic convention is that brain images are viewed from below, with the left hemisphere on the reader's right.

Example 10.3

A researcher was interested in human memory and the brain areas related to memory. The researcher hypothesized that the hippocampus would be activated by exposure to familiar surroundings but would not be activated by exposure to unfamiliar surroundings. Eighteen participants were shown pictures of their college town (familiar place), and 18 participants were shown pictures of a foreign city (unfamiliar place). All participants were right-handed college students. While participants viewed the pictures on a computer screen, their brain activity was measured with fMRI, and radiographs were used to indicate the locations of hippocampal activity (Figure 10.3).

Figure 10.3

Brain images, photomicrographs, and tissue slices are presented in a similar fashion. For photomicrographs, arrows and labels are frequently used to identify particular regions of the images.

Familiar Place   Unfamiliar Place

Figure X. Illustration of the significant difference in brain activity in the two experimental conditions. Presented are composite functional magnetic resonance imaging images (coronal slice) for 18 participants who viewed scenes from a familiar place and 18 participants who viewed scenes from an unfamiliar place. Darkened areas indicate hippocampal activity. In both conditions there was also activity (not illustrated) in other areas. R = right hemisphere; L = left hemisphere.

Checklist of Effective Elements for All Figures

- All text in figure uses the same style font (sans serif).
- Font sizes within a figure do not vary by more than 4 points.
- Text in the caption uses the same font as the text of the manuscript.
- The caption is typed double-spaced.
- Figure captions are descriptive (i.e., they describe the variables of interest and other important information, such as what abbreviations mean).
- Figure captions are listed on a separate page.
- Lines are thick enough to be clear after reduction.
- Similar figures within the same manuscript have a similar appearance.
- Figures are referred to in the text using the figure number.

Checklist of Effective Elements for Photographs

- The photograph illustrates something that would be difficult to convey with a drawing (e.g., complex 3-D stimuli, faces, body positions, brain imaging results).
- Similar photographs within the same manuscript have similar proportions.
- Contrast in the photograph is strong (for clear reproduction).

CHAPTER 11

Posters

A *poster* is a large-format presentation of a research study or theoretical paper. Most conferences have poster sessions, during which authors display posters (usually on large display boards of approximately 4 feet by 6 feet) and are available for discussion. The aim of a poster is to summarize findings in a clear, interesting way to facilitate comprehension. Ultimately, the aim is for visitors to the poster to understand what the study was about and what the results were. The more visually appealing, well organized, and informative the poster is, the more likely people are to understand the study and findings.

This chapter focuses on preparation and layout of posters that present research results. Not all posters present research results; posters presenting a theory, a model, or new apparatus, for example, would require different headings and perhaps a slightly different format than the posters described in this chapter.

Poster Preparation

Preparing a poster involves a number of decisions about what information to present and how to present that information. Making a poster involves two (possibly) conflicting goals: (a) to minimize the amount of text on the poster and (b) to make the poster easy to comprehend. To satisfy these goals, some hard decisions have to be made about what—and what not—to include.

Content Decisions

When deciding what information to include in a poster, presenters should ask themselves the following questions:

- What is the main point I want to make? Secondary points certainly can be made, but only if they really are necessary, because they add complexity to the poster.
- What are the key pieces of information people need to understand my hypotheses or arguments (e.g., previous studies, theoretical models, terms to define)? The answer to this question will decide what is presented in the first sections of the poster.
- Are there any crucial details of my methodology that need to be mentioned? This decision will be influenced by how conventional the methods are. If participants and procedures were quite typical (e.g., college undergraduates, questionnaire study), then little poster space is required for explaining them. If they are unusual, then a more lengthy explanation may be needed.
- Are there aspects of my methodology that should be illustrated with examples? It may be useful to provide examples of stimuli, questions asked of participants, rating scales used, and so forth.
- Which of my results are the most important to present? Because poster space is limited, a few key findings should be chosen to present on the poster. If a visitor is really interested in the specifics of the data, he or she can discuss it with the presenter or follow up after the conference in more detail.
- What conclusions can I realistically make? A poster presentation is not the place to speculate about the implications of research findings. Conclusions should be limited to those that are strongly supported by the data.

Style Decisions

To ensure the most efficient use of the limited poster space, presenters should ask themselves the following questions:

- How much space will I have? Many display boards provided at conferences allow posters of 4 feet (height) by 6 feet (width), but some are smaller and some are larger. The conference organizers should provide information about the dimensions.
- For every piece of information I have decided to include in the poster, can I find a way to illustrate it (with a figure) rather than describe it with text? Figures are preferable because they attract attention and often save space.
- Will my poster be printed on a series of small panels (multiple-panel format) or on one large panel (single-panel format)? With computer presentation software and access to a large format printer, it is possible to print posters on one large sheet of paper. The single-sheet or single-panel poster can be mounted easily at the conference; multiple panels have to be carefully aligned and pinned up. The disadvantages of the single-panel poster can be the cost of printing (although this varies) and the awkwardness of traveling to the conference with a poster tube (needed to protect the large poster).

Poster Layout

Conference posters have a standard layout, illustrated in Figure 11.1.

Figure 11.1

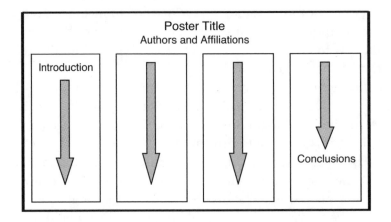

The poster title and authors' names and affiliations are presented across the top of the poster.

Figure 11.1. Standard conference poster layout.

As in this example, most posters are four columns wide. Additional columns may be permitted if there is considerable room for posters at the conference.

Text and figures are arranged in columns, starting from the top left. Presenting information in columns starting from the left allows people to read the poster without bumping into one another.

Conference posters also have a set of standard components that resemble the sections of a research article described in the *Publication Manual of the American Psychological Association.* Standard poster components include the following:

- title (with authors' names and affiliations)
- introduction (with background information, specifying research question or hypothesis)
- method (repeated for multiple experiments)
- results (repeated for multiple experiments)
- conclusions

Optional poster components include the following:

- university crest (usually placed beside authors' names)
- abstract (optional; generally printed in the conference program)
- references (optional; occupy a lot of space and could be provided in a handout)
- acknowledgments (e.g., funding agencies, research assistants)

Other Considerations

Besides the questions of content, design, and format, there are other details that need to be considered in creating an effective poster presentation. These include font style and size, use of color, numbering of sections, and creation of handouts.

Font Style and Size

Many visitors to a poster will be viewing it from several feet away. Thus, the font needs to be large and easy to read. Many veteran poster presenters recommend a sans serif font for the text (e.g., **Arial** or Helvetica) and at least 20-point type for text and 48-point type for the title.

Color

On a poster, the use of color can be very effective in catching the viewer's eye and illustrating results. The following are guidelines for using color in posters. (Chapter 12 on presentations provides information about colors and color combinations that are effective for color-blind individuals.)

- Choose two to three colors and keep them consistent throughout the poster.
- Use strong, primary colors (i.e., red, blue, and yellow). They provide the best contrast and create the most professional impression.
- Use color to highlight key words (e.g., names of conditions, important concepts) in the text. Otherwise text should be black.
- Avoid patterned backgrounds. They tend to be distracting. Most posters have a plain white background.
- Keep lots of empty (white) space on your poster to enhance the effect of colored sections.

Numbering Sections

Some poster presenters number the panels in their poster (e.g., 1, 2, 3, etc.) to help visitors follow the sequencing of the panels. Numbering panels is more likely to be useful if the poster involves multiple individual panels (rather than large single-sheet format) or if the poster deviates from the standard left-to-right layout.

Handouts

Many conference organizers require that poster presenters bring a certain number of handouts with them to the poster session. These are small, usually letter-size (8.5 x 11 in.) or legal-size (8.5 x 14 in.) versions of the poster for visitors to take away with them. To save paper, they may be double-sided. These handouts should be as similar as possible to the poster. If the poster has a single-sheet format, the handout can be a reduced version of the actual poster (the font must be large enough to be readable at this scale). If the poster uses color and the budget permits, the handouts should be printed in color.

Instead of (or in addition to) handouts, some presenters distribute diskettes containing the saved poster file, though this can be costly. Others accept business cards and mail or e-mail a copy of their poster to interested individuals. A third alternative is to post a reprint list on the poster and ask visitors who would like a copy of the poster to leave their mailing or e-mail address on the list. Many conference attendees bring address labels to the conference specifically for attaching them to reprint lists. Presenters who choose to post a reprint list have an obligation to follow through and actually mail out the reprints when they return home.

Poster Presentation

Poster presenters are usually expected to be at their poster for a certain length of time. This period could be the entire length of the poster session if the session is only a couple of hours long, or it could be a specified portion of the poster session if posters are to be on display for a longer period of time. During the poster session, many presenters stand near their poster ready to answer any questions visitors might have but let visitors read through the poster themselves. This is certainly acceptable poster-presenting behavior. As an alternative, many poster presenters prepare a short (3- to 5-min) verbal description of the study; when visitors approach the poster, the presenter asks them if they'd like to be "walked through it." Most will accept and enjoy hearing about the study (rather than reading the poster themselves). The verbal explanation should involve lots of references to the poster (e.g., "Here are the results of Experiment 1, and you can see that . . .").[1]

In addition to the poster, presenters should bring the following to the poster session:

- business cards (to give to visitors to the poster)
- thumbtacks or velcro (the conference organizers may provide these, but presenters should have their own just in case)
- notebook and pen (to jot down issues raised by visitors, to keep track of promises made to send stimuli or related papers, and so forth)
- handouts

---

1. For further information about preparing poster presentations, consult the following sources:

Briscoe, M. H. (1996). *Preparing scientific illustrations: A guide to better posters, presentations, and publications* (2nd ed.). New York: Springer-Verlag.

Gosling, P. J. (1999). *Scientist's guide to poster presentations.* New York: Kluwer Academic/Plenum Press.

Example 11.1

A researcher investigating how people's moods are influenced by the misfortunes of others devised a manipulation that involved participants hearing a person (a confederate of the experimenter) describe an unfortunate series of events (the person was ill and then caused a car accident). Half of the participants only heard about the misfortunes (they could not see the confederate but could hear him or her). The other half of the participants could both see and hear the confederate describing his or her misfortunes. The researcher hypothesized that participants' moods would be more negatively affected when they could both see and hear the confederate than when they could only hear the confederate. There was also a correlational aspect to the design: The researcher wanted to determine whether the magnitude of the mood effects was related to self-perceived driving skill.

The participants were 80 college students (40 in each exposure condition). The procedure involved a single testing session with four components: (a) Participants completed Mood Scale 1; (b) participants completed a questionnaire about a number of their skills, although the researcher was interested only in the self-ratings of driving skills; (c) the confederate "victim" arrived at the door and described his or her misfortunes to the experimenter; and (d) participants completed Mood Scale 2. The researcher examined how mood scores changed as a function of exposure to the confederate's misfortunes and also how self-perceived level of driving skill related to the extent of changes in mood. The researcher presented the findings of this study at an academic conference using the *single-panel format*, illustrated in Figures 11.2–11.9.

Exhibit 11.1

Independent Variable
1. Misfortune exposure condition (victim visible, victim not visible)

Dependent Variable
1. Reported mood

Additional Variable
1. Self-perceived driving skill

Figure 11.2

For the multiple-panel format, see Example 11.2.

When the authors have the same affiliation, the superscript letters following the names are unnecessary, and a single university is identified.

Thanks for Ruining My Day: The Effect of Misfortune on Mood

Joanne L. Mytocki[a], Jake Lalonde[b], & Mary Smith[c]

[a]Redhills College, [b]Smithton University, [c]University of the Atlantic

| Introduction | Method | Results | Conclusions |

| Research Questions | | | References |

| | | | Acknowledgments |

For optimum readability, it is best to present black text on a white background.

The empty space between sections could be a solid color other than white, but patterned backgrounds are distracting.

Figure 11.2. Overview of a single-panel poster layout.

Figure 11.3

Poster text is usually single-spaced.

Introduction

People's moods are influenced by many factors (e.g., colors, smells, music, tragic events). In experimental psychology, many mood induction techniques involve exposure to tragic events, such as reading about or viewing a negative situation (e.g., Samuels, 1989; Zeeno & Williams, 2001). This type of mood induction produces a negative mood, presumably as a result of an empathic response. This mood induction technique is typically very effective, and yet there has been little research on the conditions under which an empathic response arises. That is, under what conditions does exposure to another's misfortune have a significant effect on a person's mood? The purpose of the present research was to address this question.

In the present research, one goal was to examine the effect on mood when the victim of misfortune is visible (and not just audible). A second goal was to investigate how feelings of vulnerability relate to mood changes that occur as a result of witnessing another's misfortune.

Figure 11.3. Introduction section of sample poster.

Figure 11.4

Research Questions

1. What is the effect of *seeing the victim* on changes in mood when witnessing another person's misfortune?
2. What is the relationship of feelings of personal vulnerability to mood changes when witnessing another person's misfortune?

Figure 11.4. Research Questions section of sample poster.

Figure 11.5

Method

Participants

- 80 undergraduates
  - 40 in *victim visible* condition
  - 40 in *victim not visible* condition

Apparatus and Procedure

Events in Procedure	Time
1. Mood Scale 1	5 min
2. Skills Questionnaire (including ratings of driving skills)	20 min
3. Confederate narrative	10 min
4. Mood Scale 2	5 min

Confederate Narrative

[Confederate arrives at door of testing room and knocks. Experimenter answers the door, and confederate (agitated) says,]

"I'm signed up for your experiment today, but there is *no way* I can do it. I got up this morning and I was feeling really sick—thought I had the flu—then I was driving here and I was running late and I hit this guy's car—over at 24th Avenue—I was going through on the yellow light and I hit him, and now my car is totaled. They're towing it right now. And the other guy's car was a mess, and the cops brought me here. I should have had them take me home, but I think I'm still in shock and messed up."

Testing Room Configuration

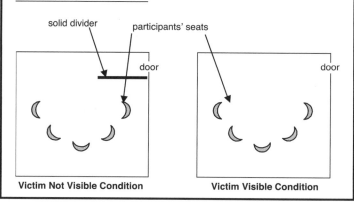

This poster might also include a photograph of the agitated confederate (with permission of the confederate).

Figure 11.5. Method section of sample poster.

Figure 11.6

Results

Figure 1. Mean mood positivity as a function of misfortune exposure condition.

Figure 2. Relationship of mood change (mood at Time 1 - mood at Time 2) to driving skill as a function of misfortune exposure condition.

Figure 11.6. Results section of sample poster.

Detailed results of statistical analyses are reported on posters only if they are central to the hypotheses.

Colored bars could be used very effectively in this figure.

If multiple figures are used, axes should be kept as consistent as possible in size, scale, and color across figures.

Color could be used in this figure to distinguish the Visible data points and line from the Not visible data points and line.

APA style for tables and figures should be followed as much as possible.

Figure 11.7

> ## Conclusions
>
> - Significant mood change occurred only when the victim of misfortune was *visible*. **Seeing (and not just hearing) someone who has been the victim of misfortune has a significant negative effect on mood.**
>
> - When participants were able to see the victim of misfortune, their change in mood was significantly related to their self-rated driving skill: Participants with lower self-ratings of driving skills tended to have stronger negative mood changes. **Feelings of vulnerability in the context of driving were related to stronger empathic responses**.
>
> - The observed relationship between driving skill and empathic responses could be caused by the more general factor of low self-esteem (manifest as low self-ratings of driving skills).

Bold text has been used here to highlight general conclusions.

Figure 11.7. Conclusions section of sample poster.

Figure 11.8

The reference list is sometimes left out if space is insufficient. It can be included in the handout.

> ## References
>
> Samuels, K. T. (1989). The effects of mood on creativity. *Journal of the Psychology of Creative Activity, 33*, 18–34.
>
> Zeeno, X. Y., & Williams, J. P. (2001). A bad case of the blues: Color preferences and mood. *Perception and Emotion, 99,* 1–31.

Reference lists on posters are often presented in a smaller font than the rest of the poster text.

Only two references are presented in this example, but there can be more than two.

Figure 11.8. References section of sample poster.

Figure 11.9

Acknowledgments

This research was supported by a grant from the Generic Research Foundation. The authors thank Greg Smith and Cameron Cox for their assistance with testing participants.

Acknowledgments can be presented in a smaller font than the rest of the poster text.

Acknowledgments can be left out if poster space is scarce. They can be included in the handouts.

Figure 11.9. Acknowledgments section of sample poster.

Example 11.2

The Example 11.1 researcher presented the results of the study at an academic conference with a *multiple-panel poster,* illustrated in Figure 11.10, rather than a single-panel poster. (Note that it is not acceptable practice to present the same study at more than one conference.) The content of individual panels was the same as in the Example 11.1 figures (11.3–11.9).

Figure 11.10

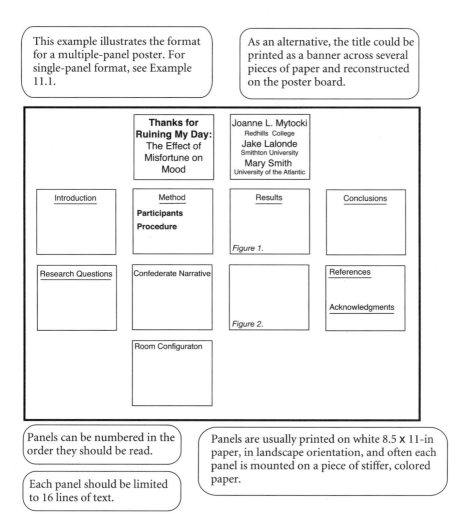

This example illustrates the format for a multiple-panel poster. For single-panel format, see Example 11.1.

As an alternative, the title could be printed as a banner across several pieces of paper and reconstructed on the poster board.

Thanks for Ruining My Day: The Effect of Misfortune on Mood

Joanne L. Mytocki
Redhills College
Jake Lalonde
Smithton University
Mary Smith
University of the Atlantic

Introduction

Method
Participants
Procedure

Results

Figure 1.

Conclusions

Research Questions

Confederate Narrative

Figure 2.

References

Acknowledgments

Room Configuraton

Panels can be numbered in the order they should be read.

Each panel should be limited to 16 lines of text.

Panels are usually printed on white 8.5 x 11-in paper, in landscape orientation, and often each panel is mounted on a piece of stiffer, colored paper.

Figure 11.10. Overview of a multiple-panel poster.

Checklist for Effective Posters

- Font type and size are consistent across panels (except where a different font is used as deliberate contrast) and across levels of headings.
- Text is large enough to be read at a distance.
- Text usually is single-spaced.
- Only text that is absolutely necessary is included; bulleted or numbered lists and replacement of text with figures save space.
- Poster panels follow a conventional sequence (e.g., Introduction, Method, Results, Conclusions).
- Each panel of a multiple-panel poster is limited to 16 lines of text.
- The color scheme is consistent.
- APA style for tables and figures as well as text is followed as closely as possible.
- If multiple figures are used, axes are consistent in size and in scale across figures where possible.
- Only key findings are presented.

CHAPTER 12

Slides and Overheads for Presentations

A presentation is a spoken description of a research study, theory, or model. There are several different types of presentations, including job talks, conference presentations, oral thesis defenses, and guest lectures. This chapter focuses on conference presentations, but many of the guidelines, tips, and examples apply to other types of presentations as well.

Conference presentations are most commonly 10 to 20 min in length, with additional time (5 to 10 min) scheduled for questions. Such presentations are usually grouped in sessions of about four to six related presentations. Conference formats do vary, however, with some involving longer talks by a few selected speakers. Conferences often have parallel sessions (several sessions of talks going on at once). Frequently, conferences include a mix of shorter and longer talks, with some parallel sessions and some keynote addresses that are scheduled alone.

Preparing Slides and Overheads for Presentations

A number of options are available to the presenter for generating presentation material. The following sections discuss the relative merits of different types of equipment and format alternatives.

Equipment

Computer

Presentation software (e.g., Microsoft PowerPoint) is often used for conference presentations. This software allows the speaker to design multiple screens for the presentation and to create a seamless presentation that includes text, figures, and video (digital video can be loaded into the presentation file). Graphics can be more sophisticated than with overhead or slide presentations, because the software provides a limitless selection of color, sound, and animations.

Presentations on a computer are not without problems. Obviously, they require a computer, which is sometimes provided by conference organizers but often must be brought by the presenter, and also a data projector (i.e., computer projector) to project the presentation from the computer screen to a larger screen. There are a number of ways this technology can fail. For instance, there can be problems connecting the computer to the data projector, problems adjusting the colors created by the data projector, and problems if the presentation is created on an IBM-compatible computer and then presented using a Macintosh computer. These problems can usually be fixed but take up valuable presentation time. Many presenters plan computer presentations but bring overheads just in case there is a technical problem.

A word of caution about computer presentations: Sometimes presenters are overzealous in their use of animation (e.g., each line of text "flies" onto the screen from different directions) or sound (e.g., each line of text is accompanied by sound effects). Overuse of animation can be distracting to the audience. The special features of computer presentation software should be used sparingly to enhance key points.

The following tips can help presenters using a computer maximize the effectiveness of their presentation:

- Practice setting up the computer and data projector.
- Use sound effects and animation only to enhance a particular point in the talk.
- If possible, use a remote mouse. This will allow you to move away from the computer while speaking.
- Make sure the room is dark enough for the projected computer screen to be visible.

- Practice going back to a particular screen in the presentation sequence. An audience member may ask a question that requires you to show a screen from the middle of the presentation. Also, during the presentation you might accidentally advance the screens and wish to back up.
- Make sure that the presentation is set to advance screens with a mouse click. Presetting a time (duration) for each screen makes the presentation hands free but also requires the presenter to stick to a very strict schedule for the presentation.

Overhead Projector

A more traditional way of presenting visual information in a conference presentation is to use overhead transparencies. An overhead projector projects the transparencies onto a larger screen visible to the audience. Many presenters like the fact that overhead projectors allow them to interact to some degree with the information on the screen: The presenter can cover up part of the transparency, exposing it only after he or she has made a particular point in the presentation (some people, however, find this annoying) or point to one part of the transparency so that the audience knows more precisely what he or she is referring to. The presenter can also use layered transparencies, in which one transparency is laid over another on the projector, with each transparency adding information. For instance, when presenting a bar graph, the first transparency could present the axes, labels, and the first bar, a second transparency could add the second bar, and so on. The transparencies can be "hinged" with tape so that they line up correctly when laid together.

Overhead presentations also have disadvantages. Many projectors distort the transparencies (they often project larger at the top than the bottom). It can be difficult to lay the transparencies straight (and the right way around) on the projector, particularly if the speaker is nervous. Transparencies have a tendency to slide off the projector; some conference organizers provide small paperweights to prevent this from happening.

The following tips can help presenters using an overhead projector maximize the effectiveness of their presentation:

- It is almost always best to use clear (rather than colored) transparencies; clear transparencies appear brighter on the screen.

- If you plan to use the same overhead at two different points in the presentation, make a second copy. It can be very difficult to find the transparency you need when it is out of sequence.
- Practice your presentation, especially placing the transparencies on the projector.
- Check that the overhead projector is in focus before you begin your presentation.
- As you place the first few transparencies on the projector during the presentation, glance over your shoulder and check that you have placed them with all text visible and in the correct orientation.

Slide Projector

A slide projector shares many characteristics of an overhead projector. The advantages of a slide projector are that, as long as the slides are loaded correctly, they are always presented straight, there is little distortion, and the presenter needs only to press a button to change slides. The disadvantage of a slide projector (as compared to an overhead projector) is that it is more difficult for the speaker to interact with the information on the screen.

Laser Pointer

A laser pointer is a hand-held device that casts a small circle of red light onto a screen. Presenters can use it to point to a particular part of a projection screen. Laser pointers must be used with caution; the beam can cause retinal damage if it is cast directly at someone's eye.

Format

Color

The use of color on slides or overheads can enhance a presentation. Strong, bright colors should be used, and cluttered backgrounds should be avoided. A consistent color theme should be used throughout the presentation. With the exception of photographs, which have many colors, no more than two or three colors should be used per screen, slide, or overhead. The following are effective color combinations that also work for people who are colorblind:

- black on white
- red on white
- turquoise on black
- magenta on black

Number of Screens, Slides, or Overheads in a Presentation

Many people find that their talk is well timed if they budget one screen, slide, or overhead for every 1 to 3 min of talk time. Each should address only one main point or issue.

Fonts

If the screens, slides, or overheads are projected onto a standard screen and the room is not too large, a font of at least 24 points should suffice for text (larger is almost always better). The font style and color should be consistent across all screens, slides, or overheads. Standard capitalization rules should be followed; text in all capital letters is difficult to read. Italics rather than bold or underlining is best to highlight points. A single style for bullet lists should be used throughout the presentation.

Text

The text on screens, slides, or overheads should be as concise as possible. The text should usually take the form of points rather than paragraphs. The text should reinforce, but not match, what the speaker is saying.

In general, screens, slides, or overheads should include at least the following (not an exhaustive list):

- author's title and affiliation and acknowledgment of collaborators
- diagram explaining the study design
- diagram explaining the procedure
- pictures of stimuli or procedure
- chart summarizing results
- conclusions[1]

1. For further information about preparing slides and overheads for presentations, consult the following sources:

Hailman, J. P., & Strier, K. B. (1997). *Planning, proposing, and presenting science*

Handouts

Handouts are used in certain disciplines (e.g., linguistics) when the stimuli and examples are quite complex. When a presenter gives the audience handouts, they can refer back to the examples throughout the talk. Many handouts include only the screens, slides, or overheads used in the presentation, plus any references. Although providing full-scale handouts is an option, a lot less paper is used (and wasted) if more than one screen, slide, or overhead is included on each page. Handouts can be an asset in talks where the presenter really wants to make a lasting impression (e.g., job talks), because audience members get something to take away with them and the presenter appears well prepared. The downside to handouts is that the audience can skip ahead, reading the handout and not paying attention to the speaker.

Handouts should include the following:

- a cover sheet with the title of the research, all authors and affiliations, and contact numbers or addresses or both
- the screens, overheads, or slides presented, as well as any additional images that would not have appeared clearly on an overhead projector, slide projector, or data (computer) projector
- efficient use of space; more than one slide or overhead is included on a single page, and handouts are printed double-sided (pages are numbered)
- references cited in the presentation

Example 12.1

A researcher was interested in autobiographical memory, particularly the nature of the events that are remembered from one's life. The researcher wanted to determine whether people's memory for events is influenced by three factors: (a) age at the time of the memory, (b) how surprising the event was, and (c) how positive the

effectively: A guide for graduate students and researchers in the behavioral sciences and biology. New York: Cambridge University Press.

Todoroff, C. (1997). *Presenting science with impact: Presentation skills for scientists, medical researchers, and health care professionals.* Toronto, Ontario, Canada: Trifolium Books.

event was. The researcher assessed the frequency of memories for four types of events: surprising positive events (e.g., winning the lottery), surprising negative events (e.g., injury in an accident), unsurprising positive events (e.g., graduating from college), and unsurprising negative events (e.g., death of a parent after a long illness). The participants were 60 individuals ages 50 to 60 years.

Testing involved two separate sessions. The first session was a personal interview in which participants were asked to recount 10 memories from each decade of their lives. In the second session, 2 days later, participants were asked to decide, for each of the memories they had recounted, whether they remembered the event as surprising or not surprising and whether they remembered it as positive or negative. The researcher prepared screens for a 15-min talk, shown in Figures 12.1–12.10.

Exhibit 12.1

Independent Variables
1. Age at time of memory (decades 0–9, 10–19, 20–29, 30–39, 40–49)
2. Surprise of event (surprising, not surprising)
3. Positivity of event (positive, negative)

Dependent Variable
1. Frequency of memories

Figure 12.1

The Good Old Days?
Investigating the Content of
Autobiographical Memories

Natalie Smith
Jordan Jones
Kate Green
Anywhere State University

The text font should be at least 24 points. The color combination should be effective and consistent.

The first author is usually (but not always) the person giving the talk.

Figure 12.1. Slide 1 of sample slide presentation.

Figure 12.2

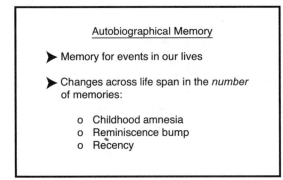

Figure 12.2. Slide 2 of sample slide presentation

Figure 12.3

Figure 12.3. Slide 3 of sample slide presentation.

Figure 12.4

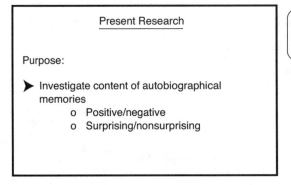

Figure 12.4. Slide 4 of sample slide presentation.

Figure 12.5

Figure 12.5. Slide 5 of sample slide presentation.

Figure 12.6

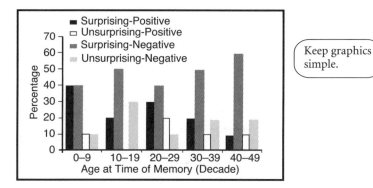

Figure 12.6. Slide 6 of sample slide presentation.

Figure 12.7

Figure 12.7. Slide 7 of sample slide presentation.

Figure 12.8

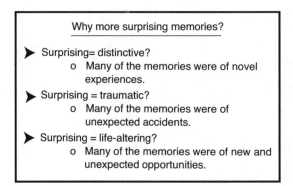

Figure 12.8. Slide 8 of sample slide presentation.

Figure 12.9

> **Why more surprising, negative memories in later decades?**
>
> ➤ Erosion of tendency to "remember the good times"?
>
> ➤ Future research required to systematically evaluate these possibilities

Figure 12.9. Slide 9 of sample slide presentation.

Figure 12.10

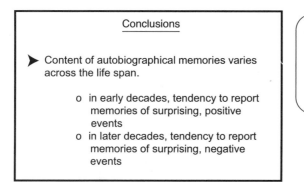

> **Conclusions**
>
> ➤ Content of autobiographical memories varies across the life span.
>
>   o in early decades, tendency to report memories of surprising, positive events
>
>   o in later decades, tendency to report memories of surprising, negative events

A reference slide would require too much text and too many slides. Presenters can provide references to the audience in a handout.

Figure 12.10. Slide 10 of sample slide presentation.

Checklist for Effective Slides and Overheads

- Font type, size, and color are consistent across slides.
- Text is large enough to be read from a distance (at least 24 points).
- There are no more than 12 lines of text per screen.
- Text is clearly organized (e.g., using bullets or numbering).
- Text is limited to that which is absolutely necessary.
- One main idea or topic is on each slide.
- Color scheme (if any) is consistent.
- Color combinations are carefully considered; bright colors give a professional appearance.
- If multiple figures are used, axes are consistent across figures where possible.
- Only key findings (those related to hypotheses and conclusions) are presented.

Index

About the Authors

ADELHEID A. M. NICOL is assistant professor in the Military Psychology and Leadership Department at the Royal Military College of Canada in Kingston, Ontario. She obtained her BSc from McGill University and her MA and PhD from the University of Western Ontario. Her interests are in the areas of honesty-integrity testing, personality testing, test construction, and legal issues in personnel selection. Dr. Nicol has taught courses in organizational behavior, research methods, social psychology, introductory psychology, and cross-cultural psychology.

PENNY M. PEXMAN is associate professor of psychology at the University of Calgary in Calgary, Alberta, Canada. She received her PhD from the University of Western Ontario in 1998. In her research she investigates the cognitive processes involved in word recognition, reading, and understanding figurative language. Dr. Pexman has taught courses in introductory psychology, cognitive psychology, sensation and perception, and educational psychology, and she is the recipient of two teaching awards.